Professor Barclay was a distinguished scholar, an exceptionally gifted preacher and a regular broadcaster. His writings for the *British Weekly* were very popular and for twenty years from 1950 a full page every week was given to them. From 1963 until 1974 he was Professor of Divinity and Biblical Criticism at Glasgow University. He was a Member of the Advisory Committee working on the New English Bible and also a Member of the Apocrypha Panel of Translators. In 1975 he was appointed a Visiting Professor at the University of Strathclyde for a period of three years where he lectured on Ethics, and in the same year—jointly with the Rev. Professor James Stewart—he received the 1975 Citation from the American theological organization The Upper Room; the first time it has been awarded outside America. His extremely popular *Bible Study Notes* using his own translation of the New Testament have achieved a world-wide sale.

Professor Barclay died in January 1978.

WILLIAM
BARCLAY

More Prayers for Plain People

ABINGDON PRESS / Nashville

MORE PRAYERS FOR PLAIN PEOPLE

Copyright © 1962 by William Barclay. All rights reserved.
Published originally in Great Britain by William Collins Sons
& Co., Ltd.
Reprinted in the U.S. by Abingdon Press,
by permission of Harper Collins Publishers.

Published by Abingdon Press in 1993 as an Abingdon Classic.
Previously published as *More Prayers for the Plain Man*,
under ISBN 0-00-623814-9.

93 94 95 96 97 98 99 00 01 02—10 9 8 7 6 5 4 3 2 1

Library of Congress Cataloging-in-Publication Data

Barclay, William, 1907–1978.
   [More prayers for the plain man]
   More prayers for plain people / William Barclay.
     p. cm.—(Abingdon classics)
   Originally published: More prayers for the plain man.
London : Wm. Collins Sons & Co., 1962.
   ISBN 0-687-27187-8
   1. Prayers. I. Title. II. Series.
BV245.B3174 1993
242'.8—dc20   92-35215
                                         CIP

MANUFACTURED IN THE UNITED STATES OF AMERICA

Contents

LORAINE D. FERGUSON

MEMORIAL

"SHE SHARED HER LOVE OF READING."

FOREWORD

It is not very long ago since *The Plain Man's Book of Prayers* first appeared in this series of Fontana Books. Since then the number of people who have read it and used it has never ceased to astonish me. And now this second volume appears. It is written in the same way, and it is intended to be used in the same way, as the first volume; but there are certain differences.

The prayers are a very little longer. I felt that those who had used the first volume, and who had formed the habit of praying every day, might want just a little more. And, therefore, in this volume the prayers are a little fuller than in the previous volume.

Prayers are given for forty mornings and for forty evenings. The reason is that I felt that it would be wise to provide some prayers which could be used as alternatives to the prayer for the day. It might be that the prayer for the day does not always express the needs, the feelings and the desires of the person who wishes to use it. And so in this volume the extra prayers will provide alternatives when the prayer of the day is not the prayer that the reader wishes to pray.

The number of prayers for special occasions and for individual people is greatly increased. Nothing will make such a difference to the ordinary, everyday routine of life as to be able to take our own particular, individual job to God. I have tried to provide prayers for those who are engaged in the many activities of the world's work. To make this complete was obviously impossible; and, if the reader should find that his or her work is not represented at all in these prayers, then I should be very happy if he or she would write to tell me so, and other prayers could be included in future editions of this book. Life would be very different, if each one of us could take the whole of life to the whole of God.

I would like to say a word about one way in which many people have found it helpful to use *The Plain Man's Book of*

Prayers. Many people found it helpful, when they were separated from their friends and loved ones, for instance, when they were in hospital, or abroad, or on holiday, or working away from home, to arrange that both they and those left at home should have a copy of the book, and to arrange that at the same time in the morning and in the evening in their different places they should together pray the same prayer. Many people have found a feeling of being together, even when they were separated, in knowing that at the same time they were offering to God the same prayer. Even though distance separated them, they met at the mercy seat of God.

I should like to think that those who use this book, unknown as they are to each other, and separated as they may be from each other, might feel themselves bound together in a praying fellowship, when morning and evening they keep their brief appointment with God.

William Barclay

WHEN WE PRAY

Sir Thomas Browne once gave to man a very strange title; he called man "the great amphibian." He meant that man is a creature of two worlds. He is a creature of this visible world of space and time, but he is also a creature of an unseen world, which every now and again breaks in upon his consciousness. Studdert Kennedy put it into verse:

I'm a man, and a man's a mixture,
Right down from his very birth,
For part of him comes from heaven,
And part of him comes from earth.

It is possible to try to explain man entirely in terms of this world. It is possible to make a chemical analysis of a man. The average man contains enough fat to make seven bars of soap; enough iron to make a medium sized nail; enough sugar to fill a sugar-sifter; enough lime to whitewash a henhouse; enough potassium to explode a toy cannon; enough magnesium for a dose of magnesia; enough phosphorus to make tips for two thousand two hundred matches; and a very little sulphur. And, as Harry Emerson Fosdick says, you could buy the whole lot for two dollars, for less than a pound. That is certainly true, but the simple answer is, Take your pound note or your two dollar bills, and go out and buy these chemicals and try to make a man. One of the curious facts which used to fascinate even the ancient Greeks is the fact that a living body and a dead body of the same person weigh exactly the same—but something is gone, and that something is the something which makes the body into a living human being, a person. Man is unquestionably a creature of two worlds.

Every now and then man becomes aware of that other world of which he also forms a part. The theologians talk of what they call the *numinous*. There are situations and places, for instance, to take the simplest example, in the dark, when a man feels that there is something there, that there is something, as it were, looking over his shoulder. At such a time a physical tremor can go through a man's body and the hair can rise on his scalp. That is the consciousness of the numinous, and that is what we might call the raw material of all religion.

This consciousness can break in upon a man anywhere, on a hilltop, on a lonely road, in the face of a sunset, in the middle of the night, in a cathedral or a church, in the face of some experience. It can come to the most irreligious man and to the most matter-of-fact man and to the man who has no contact with organised religion at all. It is part of the human situation.

This awareness of what another theologian called "the wholly other" in life comes to us especially in the times of crisis which at some time invade every life. It comes in the time of sorrow, when we know we need help from outside to go on. It comes in a time of special effort, when we know that we must pass the breaking-point and somehow not break. It comes in a time of danger in the face of which we feel helpless. That is why the sailors in Shakespeare's play say in their terror: "All's lost! To prayers! To prayers!" During the war a story used to be told of a sergeant who one evening was insisting that he was an uncompromising atheist and that he had no use whatever for any belief in God. The very next day he and some of his men were caught in a dive-bombing raid. There was nothing to do but desperately to scrabble out a fox-hole in the earth and wait. While they waited in their shallow shelter the sergeant was busy praying and praying unashamedly out loud. A soldier with him said: "I thought you were an atheist." "Son," said the sergeant, who was an honest man, "there are no atheists in fox-holes." The simple fact is that when anyone is in trouble he quite instinctively prays. That is why even the agnostic was compelled to pray, reluctantly: "O God, if there is a God, save my soul, if I have a soul!" Prayer is unquestionably the natural human reaction to a situation which has got beyond us. That is why even someone who has no connection with any church will send for someone "to say a prayer" when a member of the family is dying, and will wish a funeral service at which the prayers of the Church are said.

It needs no argument to prove that prayer is the universal reaction to any crisis and to any desperate situation. In one sense it is true to say that for many of us that is precisely our error about prayer. We tend to connect prayer with the extraordinary, the abnormal, the hour and the moment when life goes disastrously wrong, and when there is nothing that we or anyone else on earth can do about it. Of course, at such a time prayer is an absolute essential. But prayer should be an activity which is a constant part of life. If we keep prayer for the crisis, then it can happen that, when the crisis comes, we cannot pray. That is why some people have to send for someone to say a prayer for them at such a time. Prayer is simply taking life to God. Prayer is simply remembering that God is not only the rescuer when things get beyond us, but the Friend with whom we live day by day. "A man," said Dr. Johnson, "should keep his friendship in constant repair." And prayer is keeping our friendship with God in constant repair. Many people work on the unconscious assumption that they can do without God when they do not specially need him, and then call him in when everything else has failed. Certainly God will help even then, but in a time of crisis it is so much easier to go to someone who is your well-loved, constantly visited, familiar friend. And that is why prayer should be a daily activity of life. What, then, should this daily prayer be like? Let us ask and try to answer a series of questions about it.

1. *How should we pray?* The way in which we ought to pray is settled once and for all by the name which Jesus gave to God, the name by which he enabled us to address God. When Jesus was praying in Gethsemane he addressed God as: Abba, Father. Twice Paul says that that is the way in which the Christian through Christ is able to address God (Romans 8.15; Galatians 4.6). *Abba* is much more than *father*. *Abba* was the word by which a little Jewish child addressed his father in the privacy and the intimacy of the home circle, as *jaba* is in Arabic to-day. There is no way in which this can be

translated into English without it appearing bizarre and almost grotesque, for the only possible translation of *Abba* is *Daddy*. This is the way in which we can talk to God. We can talk to God with the same intimacy, and confidence, and trust as a little child talks to his father. Because of what Jesus was, because of what he told us, because of what he did, no one is easier to talk to than God.

All kinds of things are settled by this. We do not need to talk to God in any special kind of religious or theological language. Certainly we do not need to talk to him in Elizabethan and archaic English. That is why in this book I have always used *you* in speaking to God, and not *thou*. We do not need to talk to God in any special position. Kneeling, standing, sitting, lying, it is all the same. As a child runs to his father and tells him everything in the days when he is very young and very innocent and very trusting, so we can talk to God.

It is not that God is any the less God. It is simply that God for us has become the friend of all friends. Once, it is said, a Roman Emperor was celebrating a triumph. He was parading his armies, his captives and his trophies through the streets of Rome. The streets were crowded. At one place on the route there was a little platform where the Empress was sitting with her children. As the Emperor's chariot passed this place the Emperor's little son jumped down, dived through the crowd and was about to run out to the road to his father. One of the Roman legionaries who were lining the pavement stopped the boy. He swung him up in his arms. "You can't do that," he said. "Don't you know who that is? That's the Emperor." The boy looked down at him and laughed. "He may be your Emperor," he said, "but he's my father." God is God but God is *Abba* too.

We must once and for all get rid of the idea that prayer is something stilted and unnatural. It is the most natural thing in the world. It is a child talking to his father, as he did when he was very young.

II. *When should we pray?* Paul would have answered: Always and continually. "Pray without ceasing," he said (1 Thessalonians 5.17). The perfect friend is the friend to whom we can go at any time without ever feeling a nuisance. And God is like that. If God is the friend of our lives, then we will be continually speaking to him.

Should there be set times for prayer? That set times bring their own danger is clear. It is possible, as it were, to pray to a schedule, to keep, as it were, a score of the time we spend in prayer, and thus to make prayer a mechanical thing. That may be so, but it is also true that the danger about a thing which can be done any time is that it will be done no time. It is, therefore, well to have in life a fixed time for prayer, although prayer will be very far from being confined to that time. Bertram Pollock was Bishop of Norwich and as busy as a bishop must be; but, no matter how busy he was, he had three set times each day when he prayed, just as Daniel prayed three times a day with his windows open towards Jerusalem (Daniel 6.10). Once just when the Bishop was about to have his brief time of prayer a rather important visitor came asking to see him. Gently and courteously the Bishop said to his servant: "Put him in an anteroom, and ask him if he will please wait. I have an appointment with God." Daily we should have our appointment with God.

Such an appointment cannot be a formal duty; it can never be a formal duty to spend a moment or two in the company of our best friend. Such an appointment must not become a fetish. Florence Allshorn was the well-loved Principal of a women's missionary college, where sometimes there were people who observed a kind of hot-house piety; and she used to criticise gently those who always discovered that their quiet time was due just when volunteers were needed to wash the dishes! Our appointment with God must be neither a religious convention nor a religious fetish but the time without which the activities of no day are complete.

III. *Where should we pray?* Sometimes the Jews used to say that prayer was not really valid and effective unless it was offered in the Synagogue; but the great Jewish teachers also said that he who prays in his own house and home surrounds it with a wall of iron. The simple answer is that we should pray everywhere. It is quite true that there are certain places in which we are bound to feel closer to God than anywhere else. But, as Stephen said, God does not dwell in temples made with hands (Acts 7.48), and as Whittier, the Quaker poet, put it, the whole round earth is the temple of God.

We can pray anywhere, in the quiet of our own room, or, if we have not got a room of our own, on the street, in the train, on the bus, in some quiet church into which we can slip for a moment. Someone has spoken of what he called "arrow prayers," just words, phrases, half sentences spoken anywhere to God. If God is everywhere, then we can meet him anywhere. Brother Lawrence used to say that he felt just as near to God when he was washing the dirty dishes in the monastery kitchen and going about the tasks of the scullery as ever he did when he was kneeling at the Blessed Sacrament. The set appointment must be kept, but anywhere and everywhere there is a door to the presence of God which no man can ever shut.

iv. *Why should we pray?* It is here that we come to one of the misunderstandings of prayer. There are many people who think of prayer almost entirely in terms of asking God for things. Prayer can never be a monologue; prayer must be a dialogue. Prayer is at least as much listening to God as it is talking to God. Prayer is at least as much accepting the will of God as asking God for what our will desires. Prayer is a conversation between us and God, and no conversation can be worth while if one party in it never gives the other party the opportunity to speak. A good conversationalist has at least as big a gift for listening as he has for talking. There are too many people whose prayer is essentially saying to God : Your will be changed, rather than : Your will be done. In all our prayers there should be a time of silence in which we listen, for prayer is man listening to God even more than it is God listening to man. We lose far more than half the value of prayer when we speak so much that we do not even give God the chance to speak.

v. *What should we pray for?* This is a question which answers itself. The most revealing test of anything is to take it into the presence of God. The test of any wish or desire or ambition or aim is exactly this—Can I pray for it? It may often be that we see just how wrong a thing is when we realise how impossible it is to pray for it. And it may often be that our prayer must be, not to receive what we desire, but to be cleansed from desiring it. We can, in a word, pray for anything for which we can really feel that it is right to ask God.

That is not to say that there are things which we cannot bring to God. We can tell God about the temptations about which we cannot even speak to anyone else. We can tell God about the problems which we cannot share with anyone else. There are things which we try to hide from other people; and there are things in our minds and hearts from which we even try sometimes to avert our own eyes. All this we can take to God, because God, who is the searcher of the hearts of men, knows it all already, and God who in Jesus Christ took our human life upon him knows all about it.

We can pray to receive anything for which with a clear conscience and unashamedly we can ask God; and, as for the other things, we can tell God about them, and pray to be freed from the desire for them.

VI. *What can we expect from prayer?* It is here that we come to the very centre and the essence of prayer; and it is here that we come to the reason why so many people fail to make of prayer what prayer can be; it is, in fact, here that we come on the reason why so many people abandon prayer. There are two basic facts which must always be remembered about prayer.

Prayer is not escape; prayer is the way to conquest. Prayer is not flight; prayer is power. Prayer does not deliver a man from some terrible situation; prayer enables a man to face and to master the situation. When Jesus prayed that the bitter cup of the Cross might pass from him, that cup was not taken away from him. He had to drain it to its last agonising dregs. But he was enabled to come through the Cross and to emerge on the other side of it in triumph. So often people pray to be delivered from a problem, to be rescued from a situation, to be saved from a disaster, to be spared a sorrow, to be healed from a sickness, to be freed from a mental or a physical agony. Sometimes, it is true, that deliverance comes; but far more often the answer is that we are given the strength which is not our strength to go through it, and to come out at the other side of it, not simply as a survivor, but with a faith that is strengthened and deepened and a mind and a life and a character which are purified and ennobled. Prayer does not provide a means of running away from the human situation; prayer provides a way of meeting the human situation.

Prayer is not the easy way out. Prayer is not an easy way of getting things done for us. So many people think of prayer as a kind of magic, a kind of talisman, a kind of divine Aladdin's lamp in which in some mysterious way we command the power of God to work for us. Prayer must always remain quite ineffective, unless we do everything we can to make our own prayers come true. It is a basic rule of prayer that God will never do for us what we can do for ourselves. Prayer does not do things for us; it enables us to do things for ourselves.

Any wise parent knows that real parenthood does not mean doing things for the child; it means enabling the child to do things for himself. One of the great stories of history concerns Edward the First and his son the Black Prince. In battle the prince was sorely pressed. There were courtiers who came to the king to tell him that his son was up against it. " Is he wounded or unhorsed?" asked the king. When they said no, the king replied : "Then I will send him no help. Let him win his spurs." To take the matter on a much more everyday level, it is much easier for a parent, when his child asks help with a school exercise, to do the exercise and then to allow the child to copy out the answer. But by that way the child will make no progress at all. By far the wiser way is to teach and to encourage the child to do it for himself. Prayer is not so much God doing things for us as it is we and God doing things together.

We cannot expect escape from prayer, and we cannot expect the easy way out. What we can expect is a strength not our own to do the undoable, to bear the unbearable and to face the unfaceable. What we can expect is that divine help in which everything becomes victory. " In the world ye shall have tribulation," said Jesus, " but be of good cheer; I have overcome the world " (John 16.33).

Now that we have asked and tried to answer our questions about prayer, three great things remain to be said.

I. Prayer must never be selfish. There is a real sense in which no man prays as an individual, but always as a member of a community. It is for that reason that it is not enough to pray at home and by ourselves; we should also in God's house pray in fellowship and in union with God's people. No man can pray to receive something the getting of which will involve someone else's disappointment and loss. To be selfish in prayer is to erect a barrier through which our prayers cannot pass.

II. The man who prays must necessarily lift himself out of time and put himself in touch with eternity. To pray before we go out to work in the morning is to put ourselves in touch with a larger world and a larger life; it is to be lifted above the littleness of life. Robert Louis Stevenson tells of a Scottish byreman who all his life worked amidst the earthy dirt of the cowsheds and the stables. Stevenson asked the man if he never grew weary of this often unpleasant work, the same day in and day out. The man answered : " He that has something ayont need never weary." He who has something beyond need never weary. The man who prays daily puts himself in touch with that which is beyond, and comes back refreshed to life and living.

III. We have thought much of prayer as it affects ourselves; and now at the very end we think of prayer as it affects other people. The greatest thing that we can do for any man is to pray for him. Alexander Whyte told a story of a servant girl who was a member of his congregation. When she came asking to become a member, he asked her what she could do for her church and for the work of Jesus Christ. It was in the old days when the work of a domestic servant lasted all day and half the night. " I haven't much time to do things," the girl said, " but at night, when I go to bed, I take the morning newspaper with me." " Yes," said Whyte, wondering what could possibly be coming next. " And," the girl went on, " I read the birth notices, and I pray for the little babies who have just come into the world. I read the marriage notices, and I pray that God will give these people happiness.

I read the death notices, and I pray that God will comfort those who are sad." No one in this world will ever know what blessing to unknown people came from an attic bedroom from one who prayed. If we love someone, then surely we cannot help praying for them.

It is my prayer that this little book will help others to pray, and it is my prayer that they will go far beyond the words which are written in it, and that day by day they will offer their own prayers to God for themselves and for others, as a man talks with his friend.

PRAYERS WITH BIBLE READINGS
FOR FORTY MORNINGS
AND EVENINGS

FIRST DAY

In the Morning

Help me, O God, to meet in the right way and in the right spirit everything which comes to me to-day.

Help me to approach my work cheerfully, and my tasks diligently.

Help me to meet people courteously, and, if need be, to suffer fools gladly.

Help me to meet disappointments, frustrations, hindrances, opposition, calmly and without irritation.

Help me to meet delays with patience, and unreasonable demands with self-control.

Help me to accept praise modestly, and criticism without losing my temper.

Keep me serene all through to-day.

All this I ask for Jesus' sake. AMEN.

In the Evening

O God, bless those whose faces come into my mind as I come into your presence.

Bless those whom I love; if it be possible, let nothing happen to them.

Bless my friends, and the people beside whom I work; let nothing come between me and them.

Bless those whom I know to be ill; give them restful and healing sleep to-night.

Bless those whom I know to be sad; and comfort them.

Bless those who are being very foolish; keep them from doing anything that would wreck life for themselves and for others.

Bless the poor, the homeless, the friendless, those in prison, in misfortune and in disgrace.

Bless my absent friends; bless those who are away from home.

You are the Father of all. In your fatherly love bless all who need your blessing.

This I ask for your love's sake. AMEN.

Daily Reading
JOHN 1: 1-5, 11-14

In the beginning was the Word, and the Word was with God, and the Word was God. The same was in the beginning with God. All things were made by him and without him was not any thing made that was made. In him was life; and the life was the light of men. And the light shineth in darkness; and the darkness comprehended it not. He came unto his own, and his own received him not. But as many as received him, to them gave he power to become the sons of God, even to them that believe on his name: which were born, not of blood, nor of the will of the flesh, nor of the will of man, but of God. And the Word was made flesh, and dwelt among us, (and we beheld his glory, the glory as of the only begotten of the Father,) full of grace and truth.

In the Morning

O God, help me to-day to think of the feelings of others as much as I think of my own.

If I know that there are things which annoy the people with whom I live and work, help me not to do them.

If I know that there are things which would please them, help me to go out of my way to do them.

Help me to think before I speak, so that I may not thoughtlessly or tactlessly hurt or embarrass anyone else.

If I have to differ with anyone, help me to do so with courtesy.

If I have to argue with anyone, help me to do so without losing my temper.

If I have to find fault with anyone, help me to do so with kindness.

If anyone has to find fault with me, help me to accept it with a good grace.

Help me all through to-day to treat others as I would wish them to treat me: through Jesus Christ my Lord. AMEN.

In the Evening

O God, bless the people who are thinking of me and praying for me to-night,
  my parents, my family, my friends, my loved ones.

Bless those who have no one to remember them, and no one to pray for them,
  the aged, the lonely, the friendless, those who have no one to love and no one to love them.

Bless those who specially need my remembrance and my prayers,
  those in illness and in pain, those whose life is in the

balance, those who are dying, those who are in bewilder-
ment, those who are in regret and remorse, those who have
been driven to despair.

Bless me before I sleep, and grant me now
A grateful heart for all your gifts;
A contrite heart for all my sins;
A heart at peace, because it rests in you.

Hear this my prayer for your love's sake. AMEN.

Daily Reading

PSALM 46

God is our refuge and strength, a very present help in
trouble.

Therefore will not we fear, though the earth be removed, and
though the mountains be carried into the midst of the sea;

Though the waters thereof roar and be troubled, though
the mountains shake with the swelling thereof. Selah.

There is a river, the streams whereof shall make glad the
city of God, the holy place of the tabernacles of the most
High. God is in the midst of her; she shall not be moved:
God shall help her, and that right early.

The heathen raged, the kingdoms were moved: he uttered his
voice, the earth melted.

The Lord of hosts is with us; the God of Jacob is our
refuge. Selah.

Come, behold the works of the Lord, what desolations he
hath made in the earth.

He maketh wars to cease unto the end of the earth; he
breaketh the bow, and cutteth the spear in sunder; he
burneth the chariot in the fire.

Be still, and know that I am God: I will be exalted among
the heathen, I will be exalted in the earth.

The Lord of hosts is with us; the God of Jacob is our
refuge. Selah.

In the Morning

All through to-day, O God, help me to be,
    Quick to praise, and slow to criticise;
    Quick to forgive, and slow to condemn;
    Quick to share, and slow to refuse to give.

Grant me all through to-day,
    Complete control over my temper,
      that I may be slow to anger;
    Complete control over my tongue,
      that I may speak no hasty word.

So grant that all through to-day I may help everyone and hurt
no one, so that I may find true joy in living: through Jesus
Christ my Lord. AMEN.

In the Evening

O God, my Father, as I lay me down to sleep,
    Relax the tension of my body;
    Calm the restlessness of my mind;
    Still the thoughts which worry and perplex.
Help me to rest myself and all my problems in the clasp of
your everlasting arms.
Let your Spirit speak to my mind and my heart while I am

asleep, so that, when I waken in the morning, I may find that I have received in the night-time,

Light for my way;
Strength for my tasks;
Peace for my worries;
Forgiveness for my sins.

Grant me sleep to-night, and to-morrow power to live. This I ask through Jesus Christ my Lord. AMEN.

Daily Reading

MATTHEW 10: 24-31

The disciple is not above his master, nor the servant above his lord. It is enough for the disciple that he be as his master, and the servant as his lord. If they have called the master of the house Be-elzebub, how much more shall they call them of his household? Fear them not therefore: for there is nothing covered, that shall not be revealed; and hid, that shall not be known. What I tell you in darkness, that speak ye in light: and what ye hear in the ear, that preach ye upon the housetops. And fear not them which kill the body, but are not able to kill the soul: but rather fear him which is able to destroy both soul and body in hell. Are not two sparrows sold for a farthing? and one of them shall not fall on the ground without your Father. But the very hairs of your head are all numbered. Fear ye not therefore, ye are of more value than many sparrows.

In the Morning

Equip me to-day, O God, with

The humility, which will keep me from pride and from conceit;

The graciousness and the gentleness, which will make me both easy to live with and a joy to meet;

The diligence, the perseverance, and the reliability, which will make me a good workman;

The kindness which will give me a quick eye to see what I can do for others, and a ready hand to do it;

The constant awareness of your presence, which will make me do everything as unto you.

So grant that to-day men may see in me a glimpse of the life of my Blessed Lord.

This I ask for your love's sake. AMEN.

In the Evening

Thank you, O God, for all the help you have given me to-day.

Thank you for
Keeping me safe all through to-day;
Helping me to do my work all through to-day;
Giving me strength to conquer my temptations all through to-day.

Thank you for
My home and all that it has been to me;

My loved ones and all the circle of those most dear;
My friends and comrades with whom I have worked and
talked.

Thank you for
Any kindness I have received;
Any help that was given to me;
Any sympathy that was shown to me.

Help me to lay myself down to sleep to-night with a glad and
grateful heart.

This I ask through Jesus Christ my Lord. AMEN.

Daily Reading

PSALM 63: 1-7

O God, thou art my God; early will I seek thee: my soul
thirsteth for thee, my flesh longeth for thee in a dry and
thirsty land, where no water is;
To see thy power and thy glory, so as I have seen thee in the
sanctuary.
Because thy lovingkindness is better than life, my lips shall
praise thee.
Thus will I bless thee while I live: I will lift up my hands
in thy name.
My soul shall be satisfied as with marrow and fatness; and
my mouth shall praise thee with joyful lips:
When I remember thee upon my bed, and meditate on thee in
the night watches.
Because thou hast been my help, therefore in the shadow of
thy wings will I rejoice.

In the Morning

O God, help me all through to-day
  To do nothing to worry those who love me;
  To do nothing to let down those who trust me;
  To do nothing to fail those who employ me;
  To do nothing to hurt those who are close to me.

Help me all through this day
  To do nothing which would be a cause of temptation to
  someone else or which would make it easier for someone
  else to go wrong;
  Not to discourage anyone who is doing his best;
  Not to dampen anyone's enthusiasms, or to increase anyone's doubts.

Help me all through this day
  To be a comfort to the sad;
  To be a friend to the lonely;
  To be an encouragement to the dispirited;
  To be a help to those who are up against it.

So grant that others may see in me something of the reflection
of the Master whose I am and whom I seek to serve.

This I ask for your love's sake. AMEN.

In the Evening

Forgive me, O God, if to-day
  By being irritable and unreasonable, I made trouble in the
  family circle;

By being careless and slack and inefficient at my work, I
  made the tasks of others more difficult;
By being self-willed and stubborn and too set on my own
  way, I was a problem to my friends and my companions.

Forgive me if to-day
  I was too impatient with someone who was doing his best;
  I have been too quick to take offence, and to see slights
    where no slight was intended;
  I did things badly, and caused others trouble, because I was
    not attending to my instructions and to my work as I
    ought to have been.

Help me to-morrow to be more strict with myself; more understanding to others; more faithful to my work than ever before: through Jesus Christ my Lord. AMEN.

Daily Reading

MATTHEW 13: 31-34

Another parable put he forth unto them, saying, The kingdom
of heaven is like to a grain of mustard seed, which a man
took, and sowed in his field; which indeed is the least of all
seeds: but when it is grown, it is the greatest among herbs,
and becometh a tree, so that the birds of the air come and
lodge in the branches thereof. Another parable spake he unto
them: The kingdom of heaven is like unto leaven, which a
woman took, and hid in three measures of meal, till the whole
was leavened. All these things spake Jesus unto the multi-
tude in parables; and without a parable spake he not unto
them.

In the Morning

O God, I know that I am going to be very busy to-day. Help me not to be so busy that I miss the most important things.

Help me not to be too busy to look up and to see a glimpse of beauty in your world.

Help me not to be too busy listening to other voices to hear your voice when you speak to me.

Help me not to be too busy to listen to anyone who is in trouble, and to help anyone who is in difficulty.

Help me not to be too busy to stand still for a moment to think and to remember.

Help me not to be too busy to remember the claims of my home, my children, and my family.

Help me all through to-day to remember that I must work my hardest, and also to remember that sometimes I must be still.

This I ask for Jesus' sake. AMEN.

In the Evening

O God, sometimes I begin to worry, especially when I sit at the end of the day and think.

I begin to worry about my work.
Help me to know that with your help I can cope.

I begin to worry about money, and about making ends meet.

Help me to remember that, though money is important, there are things that money cannot buy—and these are the most precious things of all.

I begin to worry about my health.
Help me to remember that worrying makes me worse, and that trusting always makes me better.

I begin to worry about the things which tempt me.
Help me to remember that you are with me to help me to conquer them.

I begin to worry about those I love.
Help me to do everything I can for them, and then to leave them in your care.

Give me to-night your peace in my troubled heart: through Jesus Christ my Lord. AMEN.

Daily Reading

PSALM 51: 7-12

Purge me with hyssop, and I shall be clean: wash me, and I shall be whiter than snow.

Make me to hear joy and gladness; that the bones which thou hast broken may rejoice.

Hide thy face from my sins, and blot out all mine iniquities.

Create in me a clean heart, O God: and renew a right spirit within me.

Cast me not away from thy presence; and take not thy holy Spirit from me.

Restore unto me the joy of thy salvation; and uphold me with thy free Spirit.

In the Morning

Lord Jesus, help me to walk with you all through to-day.

Give me to-day
Something of the wisdom that was in your words;
Something of the love that was in your heart;
Something of the help that was on your hands.

Give me to-day
Something of your patience with people;
Something of your ability to bear slights and insults and injuries without bitterness and without resentment;
Something of your ability always to forgive.

Help me to live in such a way to-day that others may know that I began the day with you, and that I am walking with you, so that, however dimly, others may see you in me.

This I ask for your love's sake. AMEN.

In the Evening

O God, I think to-night of those in special trouble and distress of body, mind, or heart.

Bless the homes in which someone has died, and in which those who are left are bewildered and sad.

Bless the homes where to-night there are those who must sit by the bed of a loved one and wait for the end to come.

Bless those who are ill, and whose pain seems worst of all in the slow night hours.

Bless homes into which bad news has come, homes in which some member of the family has brought shame upon himself and sorrow to those who love him.

Bless those who are sitting alone with some bitter disappointment, with some dream that has ended, and which will now never come true.

Bless those for whom life has fallen in.

Bless those who are wrestling with some temptation, and those who have lost the battle.

Bless those who are separated from those they love, and who are lonely and anxious.

Where there is trouble of any kind, be there to comfort and support.

This I ask for your love's sake. AMEN.

Daily Reading

MATTHEW 11 : 25-30

At that time Jesus answered and said, I thank thee, O Father, Lord of heaven and earth, because thou hast hid these things from the wise and prudent, and hast revealed them unto babes. Even so, Father : for so it seemed good in thy sight. All things are delivered unto me of my Father : and no man knoweth the Son, but the Father; neither knoweth any man the Father, save the Son and he to whomsoever the Son will reveal him. Come unto me, all ye that labour and are heavy laden, and I will give you rest. Take my yoke upon you, and learn of me; for I am meek and lowly in heart; and ye shall find rest unto your souls. For my yoke is easy, and my burden is light.

In the Morning

O God, Lord of all good life, help me to use to-day well.

Help me to use to-day
To know you a little better;
To do my work a little more diligently;
To serve my fellowmen a little more lovingly;
To make myself by your help a little more like Jesus.

Help me to make to-day a day of progress in my life, and to become a little more like what you want me to be.

This I ask for Jesus' sake. AMEN.

In the Evening

Forgive me, O Father, for anything I refused to do to-day which I might have done.

Forgive me for any help I might have given to-day, and did not give.

Forgive me for being so wrapped up in my own troubles and my own problems that I had no time for those of anyone else.

Forgive me for being so immersed in my own work that I had no time to give anyone else a helping hand.

Forgive me for selfishly hoarding my own leisure and comfort, and for refusing to give them up to help others, or to help your Church and your people and your work.

Help me to learn the lesson—I know that it is true—that selfishness and happiness can never go together; and help me to find happiness in trying to forget myself, and in trying to bring help and happiness to others: through Jesus Christ my Lord. AMEN.

Daily Reading

PSALM 34: 1-8

I will bless the Lord at all times: his praise shall continually be in my mouth.

My soul shall make her boast in the Lord; the humble shall hear thereof, and be glad.

O magnify the Lord with me, and let us exalt his name together.

I sought the Lord, and he heard me, and delivered me from all my fears.

They looked unto him, and were lightened: and their faces were not ashamed.

This poor man cried, and the Lord heard him, and saved him out of all his troubles.

The angel of the Lord encampeth round about them that fear him and delivereth them.

O taste and see that the Lord is good: blessed is the man that trusteth in him.

In the Morning

Give me this day, O God,
  The energy I need to face my work;
  The diligence I need to do it well;
  The self-discipline, which will make me work just as hard,
    even if there be none to see, and none to praise, and
    none to blame;
  The self-respect which will not stoop to produce anything
    which is less than my best;
  The courtesy and the considerateness, which will make me
    easy to live with and easy to work with.

Help me so to live to-day that I may make this world a
happier place wherever I may be: through Jesus Christ my
Lord. AMEN.

In the Evening

Give me this night, O Father, the peace of mind which is
truly rest.

Take from me
  All envy of anyone else;
  All resentment for anything which has been withheld from
    me;
  All bitterness against anyone who has hurt me or wronged
    me;

All anger against the apparent injustice of life;
All foolish worry about the future, and all futile regret
about the past.

Help me to be
  At peace with myself;
  At peace with my fellowmen;
  At peace with you.

So indeed may I lay myself down to rest in peace: through
Jesus Christ my Lord. AMEN.

Daily Reading

MATTHEW 6: 27-34

Which of you by taking thought can add one cubit unto his
stature? And why take ye thought for raiment? Consider
the lilies of the field, how they grow; they toil not, neither do
they spin: and yet I say unto you, That even Solomon in all
his glory was not arrayed like one of these. Wherefore, if God
so clothe the grass of the field, which to-day is, and to-
morrow is cast into the oven, shall he not much more clothe
you, O ye of little faith? Therefore take no thought, saying,
What shall we eat? or, What shall we drink? or, Where-
withal shall we be clothed? (For after all these things do the
Gentiles seek:) for your heavenly Father knoweth that ye
have need of all these things. But seek ye first the kingdom
of God, and his righteousness; and all these things shall be
added unto you. Take therefore no thought for the morrow:
for the morrow shall take thought for the things of itself.
Sufficient unto the day is the evil thereof.

In the Morning

O God, give me strength and wisdom to live this day as I ought.

Give me
  Strength to conquer every temptation which will come to
    me;
  Strength to do every task which is assigned to me;
  Strength to shoulder every responsibility which is laid upon
    me.

Give me
  Wisdom to know when to speak, and when to keep silent;
  Wisdom to know when to act, and when to refrain from
    action;
  Wisdom to know when to speak my mind, and when to
    hold my peace.

So bring me to the end of this day in goodness, in happiness and in content: through Jesus Christ my Lord. AMEN.

In the Evening

O God, I know that there is nothing so precious as friendship and that there is nothing so enriching as love.

Thank you for all the friends whom I have met to-day.

38

Thank you for all the people with whom I travelled, with whom I walked, with whom I worked, with whom I talked, with whom I ate.

Thank you for the people with whom I listened to music, or watched plays or pictures, or watched games or played games.

Thank you for those who are even closer to me than my friends, those whom I love, and those who love me; those whose hands serve my needs and care for my comfort; those whose love surrounds me all my days.

Help me always to be loyal to my friends and true to those who love me: through Jesus Christ my Lord. AMEN.

Daily Reading

PSALM 90: 12-17

So teach us to number our days, that we may apply our hearts unto wisdom.

Return, O Lord, how long? and let it repent thee concerning thy servants.

O satisfy us early with thy mercy; that we may rejoice and be glad all our days.

Make us glad according to the days wherein thou has afflicted us, and the years wherein we have seen evil.

Let thy work appear unto thy servants, and thy glory unto their children.

And let the beauty of the Lord our God be upon us; and establish thou the work of our hands upon us; yea, the work of our hands establish thou it.

In the Morning

O God, I want to try to begin to-day by thinking not of myself but of others.

Bless those for whom to-day is going to be a difficult day:
Those who must make decisions;
Those who must wrestle with temptations;
Those who have some special problem to solve.

Bless those for whom to-day is going to be a sad day:
Those who are meeting the day with tears in their eyes and with sorrow and loneliness in their hearts;
Those who to-day must lay some dear one to rest in death;
Those who awake to the morning with no work to do.

Bless those for whom to-day is going to be a happy day:
Those who are happy and who are eagerly looking forward to to-day;
Those who are to be married to-day;
Those who will walk in the sunshine of life to-day.

Give me all through to-day sympathy and love for all, that I may always try to weep with those who weep and to rejoice with those who rejoice: through Jesus Christ my Lord. AMEN.

In the Evening

O God, I thank you for to-day.
I thank you that you gave me

Health and strength and ability to do my work;

Friends with whom to walk and talk;
Those who love me, who care for me, and who pray for me.

I thank you
For the times when you made me able to overcome my
temptations;
For the times when you made me able to choose the right
and to refuse the wrong;
For the times when you spoke to me, and gripped me, and
kept me from doing something which would have
brought me shame or regret.

I thank you for Jesus,
For his example;
For his presence with me;
For the friendship I have with you because of him.

Help me to show my gratitude by loving you more and by
serving and obeying you better: through Jesus Christ my
Lord. AMEN.

Daily Reading

JOHN 14: 1-6

Let not your heart be troubled: ye believe in God, believe
also in me. In my Father's house are many mansions: if it
were not so, I would have told you. I go to prepare a place
for you. And if I go and prepare a place for you, I will
come again, and receive you unto myself; that where I
am, there ye may be also. And whither I go ye know,
and the way ye know. Thomas saith unto him, Lord,
we know not whither thou goest; and how can we know the
way? Jesus saith unto him, I am the way, the truth, and the
life; no man cometh unto the Father, but by me.

In the Morning

O God, thank you for giving me another day, and another gift of time.

Help me all through to-day not to put off until to-morrow that which I ought to do to-day.

Help me not to put things off
Because I can't be bothered doing them;
Because I don't want to do them;
Because I don't like doing them;
Because I am afraid to do them.

Help me to do each task, to face each duty, to shoulder each responsibility as it comes to me, so that, if life should end to-night for me, there will be no loose ends, no things half-finished, no tasks undone: through Jesus Christ my Lord. AMEN.

In the Evening

When I sit down and think at night, O Father, before I go to sleep, I always feel that there never has been a day when I have done all that I meant to do, and when I have been all that I meant to be. Somehow the day is never long enough, and my strength of will is never strong enough.

Even in spite of my many failures keep me from discouragement; keep me from lowering my ideals; keep me from abandoning hope and from giving up.

Help me to try still harder; to trust still more and more in you, and less and less in myself.

This I ask for your love's sake. AMEN.

Daily Reading

PSALM 95: 1-6

O come, let us sing unto the Lord : let us make a joyful noise to the rock of our salvation.

Let us come before his presence with thanksgiving, and make a joyful noise unto him with psalms.

For the Lord is a great God, and a great King above all gods.

In his hand are the deep places of the earth : the strength of the hills is his also.

The sea is, and he made it : and his hands formed the dry land.

O come, let us worship and bow down : let us kneel before the Lord our maker.

In the Morning

O God, my Father, I am very fortunate in my home, my parents, my family, my friends, my work, my church, my country. To-day, before I go out to work, I want to remember before you those for whom life is not nearly so happy as it is for me,

Refugees who have no home, no place to call their own;
Coloured people in lands in which coloured people have no rights;
Those who love freedom in lands where freedom is lost;
Christians in lands where Christians are persecuted;
Those who are unhappy in their work, badly paid, compelled to work in bad conditions;
Those who are treated at home without sympathy, and even with cruelty;
Those who live or work in a situation in which it is very difficult to be a Christian at all;
The friendless, the lonely, and the sad;
Those in hospitals and in places for those whose minds have lost the light of reason;
Those in prison and in disgrace.

O God, grant that my own happiness may never make me blind to the need and forgetful of the unhappiness of others: This I ask for your love's sake. AMEN.

In the Evening

Forgive me, O God,
If to-day I have been too impatient, especially with people;

If to-day I have made anyone feel a nuisance;
If to-day in my heart of hearts I have thought people fools
—and have shown them that I did;
If to-day there were times when I was too aggressively sure
that I was right;
If to-day I have ridden rough-shod over the feelings of
someone else;
If to-day I have been
Unapproachable to talk to;
Difficult to work with;
Unsympathetic to appeal to;
Critical in my outlook;
Harsh in my judgment.

I cannot undo what I have done, but help me to-morrow to be
more loving and more kind—more like Jesus.

This I ask for your love's sake. AMEN.

Daily Reading

JOHN 15: 1-5

I am the true vine, and my Father is the husbandman. Every
branch in me that beareth not fruit he taketh away; and every
branch that beareth fruit, he purgeth it, that it may bring
forth more fruit. Now ye are clean through the word which
I have spoken unto you. Abide in me and I in you. As the
branch cannot bear fruit of itself, except it abide in the vine;
no more can ye, except ye abide in me. I am the vine, ye are
the branches: he that abideth in me, and I in him, the same
bringeth forth much fruit: for without me ye can do nothing.

45

In the Morning

O God, my Father, as I go out to life and work to-day,

I thank you for the world's beauty:
For the light of the sun;
For the wind on my face;
For the colour of the flowers;
And for all glimpses of lovely things.

I thank you for life's gracious things:
For friendship's help;
For kinship's strength;
For love's wonder.

I remember this world's evil and its sin.
Help me to overcome every temptation, and make my life
like a light which guides to goodness. And, if anyone
has fallen, help me to sympathise and to help rather
than to judge and condemn.

I remember this world's sorrow.
Help me to-day to bring comfort to some broken heart,
and cheer to some lonely life.

So grant that, when evening comes, I may feel that I have
not wasted this day.

Hear this my prayer through Jesus Christ my Lord. AMEN.

In the Evening

O God, my Father, to-night I bring to you myself, my life and all that is in it.

I bring to you
My sins for your forgiveness;
My hopes, my aims, my ambitions for your blessing;
My temptations for your strength;
My tasks, my duties, my responsibilities for your help;
My friends, my dear ones, my loved ones for your care and your protection;
And I bring everything with a thankful and a grateful heart for all that you have done for me.

So grant to me to sleep to-night with the everlasting arms underneath and about me: through Jesus Christ my Lord. AMEN.

Daily Reading

PSALM 100

Make a joyful noise unto the Lord, all ye lands.
Serve the Lord with gladness : come before his presence with singing.
Know ye that the Lord he is God : it is he that hath made us, and not we ourselves; we are his people, and the sheep of his pasture.
Enter into his gates with thanksgiving, and into his courts with praise : be thankful unto him, and bless his name.
For the Lord is good : his mercy is everlasting; and his truth endureth to all generations.

In the Morning

O God, my Father, keep me from all failure all through to-day.

Keep me from
Failure in gratitude to those to whom I owe so much;
Failure in diligence to those to whom I owe my duty and my work;
Failure in self-control, when temptation comes and when passions are strong.

Keep me from
Failure to give my help to those who need my help;
Failure to give an example and a lead to those who need support in goodness;
Failure in kindness to those who are in trouble of any kind.

Help me this day perfectly to fulfil my responsibilities to myself, to my loved ones, to my employers, to my fellowmen and to you.

This I ask for Jesus' sake. AMEN.

In the Evening

O God, you are the Father of all, and I ask your blessing on all those who are in trouble to-night.

I ask you to bless and help
Little children who are afraid of the dark;
Sufferers who cannot sleep for their pain;
Those who in sorrow are lonelier than ever they thought it possible to be.

I ask you to bless and help
Those in prison and in disgrace;

Those who have suddenly realised the mess they have made of life for themselves and for others;

Those who have been hurt, wounded, failed, by those whom they trusted, those in whom they believed, those whom they loved;

Those who have newly come to see the sorrow and the heartbreak of which their thoughtlessness has been the cause.

O God, my Father, bless me now before I sleep.

Thank you for to-day and for all the happy things that were in it.

Forgive me for anything in it which was wrong, and which grieved others or hurt you.

Give me now a good night's rest and quiet sleep.

This I ask for Jesus' sake. AMEN.

Daily Reading

LUKE 9: 57-62

And it came to pass, that, as they went in the way, a certain man said unto him, Lord, I will follow thee whithersoever thou goest. And Jesus said unto him, Foxes have holes, and birds of the air have nests; but the Son of man hath not where to lay his head. And he said unto another, Follow me. But he said, Lord, suffer me first to go and bury my father. Jesus said unto him, Let the dead bury their dead: but go thou and preach the kingdom of God. And another also said, Lord, I will follow thee; but let me first go bid them farewell, which are at home at my house. And Jesus said unto him, No man, having put his hand to the plough, and looking back, is fit for the kingdom of God.

In the Morning

Eternal and everblessed God, whom to know is life eternal,

Help me daily to know you better, that daily I may more fully enter into real life, and may more fully know the meaning of life.

Eternal and everblessed God, whom to serve is perfect freedom,

Grant that I may daily serve you more faithfully, so that in doing your will I may find my peace.

Eternal and everblessed God, whom to love is fulness of joy,

Help me day by day to love you more, so that I may come a little nearer to loving you as you first loved me.

Hear this my prayer, through Jesus Christ my Lord. AMEN.

In the Evening

O God, forgive me for allowing any wrong thoughts to enter into my mind to-day.

Forgive me for allowing my eyes to linger on things at which I should not even have looked.

Forgive me for speaking words which I should never have allowed to soil my lips.

———————

Forgive me for needlessly giving temptation a chance to attack me.

Forgive me for all the things for which I am sorry now, and grant to me, before I sleep, the sense of being forgiven and the kiss of pardon and of peace.

This I ask for your love's sake. AMEN.

Daily Reading

PSALM 124

If it had not been the Lord who was on our side, now may Israel say;

If it had not been the Lord who was on our side, when men rose up against us:

Then they had swallowed us up quick, when their wrath was kindled against us:

Then the waters had overwhelmed us, the stream had gone over our soul:

Then the proud waters had gone over our soul.

Blessed be the Lord, who hath not given us as a prey to their teeth.

Our soul is escaped as a bird out of the snare of the fowlers; the snare is broken, and we are escaped.

Our help is in the name of the Lord, who made heaven and earth.

In the Morning

O God, Father and Protector of all, bless all those for whom this will be a worrying and a difficult day:

People in hospital, waiting to undergo an operation to-day;

People who must take some very important decision to-day;

Scholars at school, students at university, who must sit some examination to-day;

Those who are leaving home for the first time to-day, to go to some place that is new and strange, and people who are beginning a new job to-day;

Those who have to face some interview to-day, the result of which will make a very big difference to them;

Those for whom to-day

Work will be specially hard;

Temptation will be specially strong;

People will be specially difficult.

Bless all such people, and bless me. Grant that they and I may be so strengthened and guided that we may come to the end of the day with no mistakes and with no regrets: through Jesus Christ my Lord. AMEN.

In the Evening

O God, I thank you for the things which I have discovered to-day:

For any new thing which I know now which I did not know this morning;

For anything that has been added to my store of knowledge and of experience;

For books that I have read and places that I have seen:
I thank you, O God.

I thank you for all the people I have discovered to-day:
For the friends I have known for long;
For new acquaintances whom I have made;
For people I met who have the same interests as I have, and
to whom it was a joy to talk:
I thank you, O God.

I thank you specially for people whom I did not like and
whom now for the first time I am beginning to understand.

Amidst all the changes of life I thank you for Jesus who is
always the same, yesterday, to-day and forever.

Hear this my evening thanksgiving, and help me to try to
deserve it all a little better: through Jesus Christ my Lord.
AMEN.

Daily Reading

LUKE 10: 38-42

Now it came to pass, as they went, that he entered into a
certain village: and a certain woman named Martha received
him into her house. And she had a sister called Mary, which
also sat at Jesus' feet, and heard his word. But Martha was
cumbered about much serving, and came to him, and said,
Lord, dost thou not care that my sister hath left me to serve
alone? bid her therefore that she help me. And Jesus
answered and said unto her, Martha, Martha, thou art careful
and troubled about many things: but one thing is needful:
and Mary hath chosen that good part, which shall not be taken
away from her.

In the Morning

O God, bless all those who have very responsible jobs to do to-day:

Teachers who mould the minds and lives of boys and girls;

Doctors and surgeons whose skill makes people well again and eases their pain;

Lawyers who interpret the law, policemen who enforce the law, judges who administer justice;

Those in whose employment and control there are many workers, and whose decisions affect many lives;

Those on the roads, on the railways, at sea, and in the air, in whose hands are the lives and the safety of those who travel and journey;

Scientists who control decisions and discover powers which can bring life and death;

Statesmen whose decisions affect the welfare of the nations and of the world;

Preachers who tell the story of Jesus in this land and in lands across the sea;

Parents to whom there has been given the privilege and the responsibility of a child.

Help them and support them in their work, and help me to-day to do well every task, however humble, which is given me to do: through Jesus Christ my Lord. AMEN.

In the Evening

O God, forgive me for all to-day's mistakes.

When I look back, I think of
The things I would do much better, if I had the chance to do them again;

The people to whom I would be so much kinder and so much more courteous, if I could meet them again;

The things that I wish I had not done, and the words that I wish I had not spoken;

The things I failed to do, and the chance to do which may never come back again;

The fine impulses which I would turn into action, if I had to-day again.

O God, give me sleep to-night; and in the days to come give me strength and grace to do what I know I ought to do, and to live in the way I know I ought to live: through Jesus Christ my Lord. AMEN.

Daily Reading

PSALM 136: 1-5, 23-26

O give thanks unto the Lord; for he is good: for his mercy endureth for ever.

O give thanks unto the God of gods: for his mercy endureth for ever.

O give thanks to the Lord of lords: for his mercy endureth for ever.

To him who alone doeth great wonders: for his mercy endureth for ever.

To him that by wisdom made the heavens: for his mercy endureth for ever.

Who remembered us in our low estate: for his mercy endureth for ever.

And hath redeemed us from our enemies: for his mercy endureth for ever.

Who giveth food to all flesh: for his mercy endureth for ever.

O give thanks unto the God of heaven: for his mercy endureth for ever.

In the Morning

O God, my Father, give me patience all through to-day.

Give me patience with my work,
   so that I may work at a job until I finish it or get it right,
   no matter how difficult or how boring it may be.

Give me patience with people,
   so that I will not become irritated or annoyed,
   and so that I may never lose my temper with them.

Give me patience with life,
   so that I may not give up hope
   when hopes are long in coming true;
   so that I may accept disappointment without bitterness
   and delay without complaint.

Hear this my morning prayer for your love's sake. AMEN.

In the Evening

O God, as I lay myself down to rest to-night, I pray for all those who do not like the night;

   Bless little children who are afraid of the dark.

Bless those in illness and in pain, for whom the night
hours are very slow and very long.

Bless those who are lonely, and who in the stillness of the
night feel their loneliness all the more.

Bless those who are sad, and who in the night time miss
someone who is gone from them more than at any other
time.

Bless those who are away from home in hospitals and in
infirmaries, in journeyings and in distant places.

Bless those who are worried, and whose thoughts will not
let them sleep.

O God, give me to-night a heart content and a mind at rest,
so that I may sleep in peace and rise in strength: through
Jesus Christ my Lord. AMEN.

Daily Reading

JOHN 10: 7-11

Then said Jesus unto them again, Verily, verily, I say unto
you, I am the door of the sheep. All that ever came before
me are thieves and robbers: but the sheep did not hear them.
I am the door: by me if any man enter in, he shall be saved,
and shall go in and out, and find pasture. The thief cometh
not, but for to steal, and to kill, and to destroy: I am come
that they might have life, and that they might have it more
abundantly. I am the good shepherd: the good shepherd
giveth his life for the sheep.

In the Morning

O God, grant that to-day
  I may not disappoint any friend;
  I may not grieve any loved one;
  I may not fail anyone to whom I have a duty;
  I may not shame myself.

Grant that to-day
  I may do my work with honesty and fidelity;
  I may take my pleasure in happiness and purity.

Grant that to-day
  I may lead no one astray;
  I may not make goodness and faith harder for anyone.

Help me to-day to be a help and example to all, and to bring strength and encouragement, wherever I may be: through Jesus Christ my Lord. AMEN.

In the Evening

O God, at the end of the day it is not so much the things that I have done which worry me as the things which I have not done.

Forgive me for the tasks into which I did not put my best, for work that was shoddy, and for workmanship of which any true craftsman would be ashamed.

Forgive me for the things I did not do, and for the help I did not give.

Forgive me for the word of praise and the word of thanks I did not speak.

Forgive me for my failure in courtesy and in graciousness to those with whom I live and work.

Help me each day to do better, so that each night I may have fewer regrets: through Jesus Christ my Lord. AMEN.

Daily Reading

ISAIAH 6: 1-8

In the year that king Uzziah died I saw also the Lord sitting upon a throne, high and lifted up, and his train filled the temple. Above it stood the seraphim: each one had six wings; with twain he covered his face, and with twain he covered his feet, and with twain he did fly. And one cried unto another, and said, Holy, holy, holy, is the Lord of hosts: the whole earth is full of his glory. And the posts of the door moved at the voice of him that cried, and the house was filled with smoke. Then said I, Woe is me! for I am undone; because I am a man of unclean lips, and I dwell in the midst of a people of unclean lips: for mine eyes have seen the King, the Lord of hosts. Then flew one of the seraphim unto me, having a live coal in his hand, which he had taken with the tongs from off the altar: and he laid it upon my mouth, and said, Lo, this hath touched thy lips; and thine iniquity is taken away, and thy sin purged. Also I heard the voice of the Lord, saying, Whom shall I send, and who will go for us? Then said I, Here am I; send me.

In the Morning

O God, help me to-day and every day to use life as you would have me to use it.

Help me to use whatever gifts and whatever strength I have to help others, and to make a useful contribution to the life and the work of the world, wherever I am.

Help me to use whatever money I have, not selfishly, but generously.

Help me to use my time wisely in honest work; help me to use my spare time, not altogether selfishly, and not altogether for my own pleasure, but to do something in it for others.

Help me to use my mind to get new knowledge and to improve myself; help me never to stop learning, and not to be entirely taken up with light and frivolous things.

Help me to use to-day in such a way that in it I may improve myself, help others and please you: through Jesus Christ my Lord. AMEN.

In the Evening

O God, when I sit and think at the end of the day, I realise how unsatisfactory I am.

So often I do not give my employers my best work.

So often I only make use of my home, and I am more disobliging and more discourteous to those who love me most than to anyone else.

So often I expect far more from my friends than I am prepared to give to them.

So often I find pleasure in things in which I shouldn't.

So often I allow thoughts and pictures to come into my mind, and feelings to come into my heart, which should never be allowed to find an entry there.

So often I refuse to give my Church the help and the service I could well give, even if it does mean giving up something of my time or money.

So often I shirk work, evade decisions, refuse duties, and run away from responsibilities.

Forgive me, O God. Help me to try harder and to do better. Give me your strength to do the things which I cannot do myself. This I ask for Jesus' sake. AMEN.

Daily Reading

2 CORINTHIANS 5: 17-21

Therefore if any man be in Christ, he is a new creature: old things are passed away; behold, all things are become new. And all things are of God, who hath reconciled us to himself by Jesus Christ, and hath given to us the ministry of reconciliation; to wit, that God was in Christ, reconciling the world unto himself, not imputing their trespasses unto them; and hath committed unto us the word of reconciliation. Now then we are ambassadors for Christ, as though God did beseech you by us: we pray you in Christ's stead, be ye reconciled to God. For he hath made him to be sin for us, who knew no sin; that we might be made the righteousness of God in him.

In the Morning

O God, this morning I have come into the quietness and stillness of your presence to begin the day, so that out of this
moment I may take with me a quiet serenity which will last
me through the rough and tumble of this day's life.

I have come to find wisdom,
  so that to-day I may not make any foolish mistakes.

I have come to find peace,
  so that nothing may worry or upset me all through to-day.

I have come to find love,
  so that all through to-day nothing may make me bitter or
  unforgiving or unkind.

I have come to begin the day with you, to continue it with
you, and to end it with you, so that it will be a day which will
have in it nothing to regret.

Hear this my morning prayer for Jesus' sake. AMEN.

In the Evening

O God, I started out to-day with all kinds of high hopes and
resolutions, but it has just been another of these days.

I have been just as easily irritated and annoyed as ever I
  was.

I have been just as easily worried and flustered and upset as
  ever I was.

I have been just as impatient with people, just as quick in temper and tongue as ever I was.

I have been no kinder, no more considerate, no more like Jesus.

O God, it would be easy to make excuses, to put the blame on others, to say that it was not all my fault. But I don't want to say that, because it would not really be true. All I want to say is: Forgive me, help me not to be discouraged, and not to give up the battle for goodness, and help me to do better to-morrow.

All this I ask for your love's sake. AMEN.

Daily Reading

ISAIAH 53: 1-6

Who hath believed our report? and to whom is the arm of the Lord revealed? For he shall grow up before him as a tender plant, and as a root out of a dry ground: he hath no form nor comeliness; and when we shall see him, there is no beauty that we should desire him. He is despised and rejected of men, a man of sorrows, and acquainted with grief: and we hid as it were our faces from him; he was despised, and we esteemed him not. Surely he hath borne our griefs, and carried our sorrows: yet we did esteem him stricken, smitten of God, and afflicted. But he was wounded for our transgressions, he was bruised for our iniquities: the chastisement of our peace was upon him; and with his stripes we are healed. All we like sheep have gone astray; we have turned every one to his own way; and the Lord hath laid on him the iniquity of us all.

In the Morning

O God, you know me, and you know that I don't want to go out at all to-day.

> I am tired before I start. There are people I don't want to meet; there are jobs I don't want to do. There are tasks which I will have to do, and I am not nearly as well prepared for them as I ought to be.

> I would much rather stay at home, or run away from it all. But I can't do that, and I know I can't do that.' I know quite well life has got to go on, no matter how I feel about it.

Lord Jesus, come with me, and help me to feel you beside me all day, so that I will not only get grimly through to-day, but that I may know the joy of living with you.

This I ask for your love's sake. AMEN.

In the Evening

O God, bless all my friends and my loved ones to-night.

Bless those whose lives are interwoven with mine, and without whom life could never be the same. Bless those to whom I owe my comfort, and without whom life would be very lonely.

Bless the one to whom I have given my heart to keep, and who has given me his/her heart to keep, and keep us for ever loyal, for ever loving, and for ever true to one another.

Bless my absent friends and loved ones, from whom for a time I am separated. Guard them, guide them, protect them, and grant that we may soon meet again.

I know that all for whom I am praying are also praying for me. Help me just now to feel very near to them, and not only to them, but even to those whom I have loved and lost awhile, and who have gone to be with you.

Hear this my prayer for your love's sake. AMEN.

Daily Reading

I CORINTHIANS 3: 18-23

Let no man deceive himself. If any man among you seemeth to be wise in this world, let him become a fool, that he may be wise. For the wisdom of this world is foolishness with God. For it is written, He taketh the wise in their own craftiness. And again, The Lord knoweth the thoughts of the wise, that they are vain. Therefore let no man glory in men. For all things are yours; whether Paul, or Apollos, or Cephas, or the world, or life, or death, or things present, or things to come; all are yours; and ye are Christ's; and Christ is God's.

In the Morning

O God, my Father, make me more appreciative of others.

Help me never to fail to say thanks for everything that is done for me, and never to take anything for granted, just because it comes to me unfailingly every day.

Help me always to be ready to speak a word of praise, whenever a word of praise is possible—and sometimes even when it is not possible.

Help me to be quick to notice things. Help me to be quick to see when someone is depressed and discouraged and unhappy. Help me to be quick to see it when someone is lonely and shy and is left out of things.

O Lord Jesus, all through to-day help me to see people with your eyes.

This I ask for your love's sake. AMEN.

In the Evening

Forgive me, O God, for all the trouble I have caused to-day.

Forgive me
if I made a nuisance of myself by being stupidly obstinate, or needlessly obstructive, or foolishly fussy.

Forgive me
if I have caused other people trouble by keeping them waiting for me, or by being late with my work, or by failing to keep a promise.

Forgive me
> if I have annoyed others by trying to be funny at the wrong time, by making jokes about the wrong things, or by being cross, irritable, bad-tempered, discourteous.

Forgive me
> if I could see no point of view but my own, or if I was hard to work with, or difficult to live with.

To-night, O God, forgive me. To-morrow is another day; help me to make a better job of it than I did of to-day.

This I ask for your love's sake. AMEN.

Daily Reading

ISAIAH 55: 6-11

Seek ye the Lord while he may be found, call ye upon him while he is near: let the wicked forsake his way, and the unrighteous man his thoughts: and let him return unto the Lord, and he will have mercy upon him: and to our God, for he will abundantly pardon. For my thoughts are not your thoughts, neither are your ways my ways, saith the Lord. For as the heavens are higher than the earth, so are my ways higher than your ways, and my thoughts than your thoughts. For as the rain cometh down, and the snow from heaven, and returneth not thither, but watereth the earth, and maketh it bring forth and bud, that it may give seed to the sower, and bread to the eater: so shall my word be that goeth forth out of my mouth: it shall not return unto me void, but it shall accomplish that which I please, and it shall prosper in the thing whereto I sent it.

In the Morning

O God, so help me to-day that nothing may make me lose my temper.

So help me that nothing may make me lose my serenity, that I may be proof alike against the big blows and the petty pinpricks of life.

So help me that nothing may make me lose my patience either with things or with people.

So help me that I may not get flustered or excited, but that I may take things easily and just as they come.

So help me to work that I may do things when they ought to be done, and as they ought to be done, so that there will be no last-minute rush to-day.

So help me that nothing may make me take offence or differ in bitterness with anyone to-day.

To-day, O God, garrison my heart with your peace and equip my life with your strength.

This I ask for your love's sake. AMEN.

In the Evening

Forgive me, O God,
if I have behaved to-day as if I was the only person who was busy, and as if I was the only person who had a lot to do.

Forgive me
    if I have behaved as if I was the only person for whom
    things were difficult and hard, and as if life was unkinder
    to me than to anyone else.

Forgive me
    if I have behaved as if I was the only person who was mis-
    judged or misunderstood, and as if I was the only person
    who ever got a raw deal.

Forgive me for magnifying my troubles and for forgetting
    my blessings.
Help me from now on to get things in their right proportions
by thinking far more of others and far less of myself.

This I ask for your love's sake. AMEN.

Daily Reading

I CORINTHIANS 15: 53-58

For this corruptible must put on incorruption, and this mortal
must put on immortality. So when this corruptible shall have
put on incorruption, and this mortal shall have put on immortality, then shall be brought to pass the saying that is
written, Death is swallowed up in victory. O death, where
is thy sting? O grave, where is thy victory? The sting of
death is sin; and the strength of sin is the law. But thanks
be to God, which giveth us the victory through our Lord
Jesus Christ. Therefore, my beloved brethren, be ye stead-
fast, unmoveable, always abounding in the work of the Lord,
forasmuch as ye know that your labour is not in vain in the
Lord.

In the Morning

O God, my Father, give me to-day
Courage, to do the things I am afraid to do;
Conscientiousness, to do the things I do not want to do;
Grace to get alongside the people I do not like and who
do not like me.

Grant that even in the dull routine of the day's work I may
find a thrill, because I remember that I am doing it with you,
so that even the uninteresting things may become interesting,
and so that even things which seem not to matter may become
important.

Help me to be happy all through to-day, and to make others
happy too.

This I ask for Jesus' sake. AMEN.

In the Evening

O God, I thank you for to-day.

I thank you
that I was able to do the work which earns the pay to
support myself and those whom I love and who are depen-
dent on me.

I thank you
for the people I met, and whose company I enjoyed.

I thank you
    for any temptation you made me able to overcome;
    for any new thing which I have learned;
    for any useful thing I was able to do;
    for anyone I know better, and to whom I have come closer
      to-day.

Help me now to go to sleep with a quiet mind, and to wake to-morrow glad to meet another day: through Jesus Christ my Lord. AMEN.

Daily Reading

JEREMIAH 31: 31-34

Behold the days come, saith the Lord, that I will make a new covenant with the house of Israel, and with the house of Judah: not according to the covenant that I made with their fathers in the day that I took them by the hand to bring them out of the land of Egypt; which my covenant they brake, although I was a husband unto them, saith the Lord: but this shall be the covenant that I will make with the house of Israel: After those days, saith the Lord, I will put my law in their inward parts, and write it in their hearts; and will be their God, and they shall be my people. And they shall teach no more every man his neighbour, and every man his brother, saying, Know the Lord: for they shall all know me, from the least of them unto the greatest of them, saith the Lord: for I will forgive their iniquity, and I will remember their sin no more.

In the Morning

I thank you, O God, for health and strength to go out and to do my work; and I remember before you those who cannot go out to work to-day.

I remember
 Those who are ill and in pain at home and in the hospitals and the infirmaries and nursing-homes;
 Those who are helpless and paralysed;
 Those whose nerves and minds have collapsed under the strain of living;
 Those who are slowly recovering from a long illness.

I remember
 Those who are old, and whose day's work is done, and who are feeling useless;
 Those who are in disgrace;
 Those who are unemployed, and who have no work to do, and who are worried about what is to happen to their homes and to their loved ones.

Bless all the people who are like that. And, even if my work is dull, or worrying, or hard, or badly paid, or unappreciated, help me to remember how fortunate I am to have the health and strength to do it, and help me not to forget to be grateful to you.

This I ask for Jesus' sake. AMEN.

In the Evening

O God, help me to-night to relax in body and in mind.

Take from me the tension which makes rest impossible.

Take from me the worries which fill my mind with thoughts which destroy sleep.

Take from me the fears which lurk at the back of my mind, which come to haunt me when work is laid aside, and when there is too much time to think.

Help me to-night really and truly to cast my care upon you, really and truly to feel the everlasting arms underneath and about me.

Help me to sleep to-night, not just the sleep of tiredness, but the sleep of peace; through Jesus Christ my Lord. AMEN.

Daily Reading

2 CORINTHIANS 12: 7-10

And lest I should be exalted above measure through the abundance of the revelations, there was given to me a thorn in the flesh, the messenger of Satan to buffet me, lest I should be exalted above measure. For this thing I besought the Lord thrice, that it might depart from me. And he said unto me, My grace is sufficient for thee: for my strength is made perfect in weakness. Most gladly therefore will I rather glory in my infirmities, that the power of Christ may rest upon me. Therefore I take pleasure in infirmities, in reproaches, in necessities, in persecutions, in distresses for Christ's sake: for when I am weak, then am I strong.

73

In the Morning

O God, give me the things which will make me able to live well to-day.

Give me
A sense of proportion,
that I may see what is important and what is not important, and that I may not get all hot and bothered about things which do not matter;

A sense of humour,
that I may learn to laugh,
and especially to laugh at myself, and not to take myself too seriously;

A sense of responsibility,
that I may look on each task as something which I am doing for the general good and for you.

Give me
A new sensitiveness of spirit,
that I may see when I am hurting people,
and that I may not blindly and thoughtlessly trample on the feelings of others.

Give me, too, a continual awareness of the presence of Jesus, that I may do nothing which it would grieve him to see, and nothing which it would hurt him to hear.

This I ask for your love's sake. AMEN.

In the Evening

O God, I thank you for to-day.

I thank you for any lovely thing that I have seen or experienced.

I thank you for anything which happened to me which made me feel that life is really and truly worth living.

I thank you for all the laughter which was in to-day.

I thank you, too, for any moment in which I saw the seriousness and the meaning of life.

I thank you very specially for those I love, and for those who love me, and for all the difference it has made to me to know them, and for all the happiness it brings to me to be with them.

O God, my Father, forgive me for anything in to-day which has vexed others, which has shamed myself, which has disappointed my friends, or which has grieved you.

Give me the sense of being forgiven, that I may lay me down to sleep in peace: through Jesus Christ my Lord. AMEN.

Daily Reading

JOEL 2: 28-32

And it shall come to pass afterward, that I will pour out my spirit upon all flesh: and your sons and your daughters shall prophesy, your old men shall dream dreams, your young men see visions: and also upon the servants and upon the handmaids in those days will I pour out my spirit. And I will shew wonders in the heavens and in the earth, blood, and fire, and pillars of smoke. The sun shall be turned into darkness, and the moon into blood, before the great and the terrible day of the Lord come. And it shall come to pass, that whosoever shall call on the name of the Lord shall be delivered: for in mount Zion and in Jerusalem shall be deliverance, as the Lord hath said, and in the remnant whom the Lord shall call.

In the Morning

O God, all through to-day make me quicker to praise than to criticise.

Help me never to forget to thank people for anything that they do for me.

Make me always ready to speak a word of praise and of appreciation.

Grant that I may take no service for granted, and that I may allow no help to pass unnoticed.

Make me quick to notice when people are upset or depressed, and give me the ability to speak the word which will help and cheer them.

All through to-day help me to think far less of myself and far more of others, and so to find my own happiness in making others happy.

This I ask for Jesus' sake. AMEN.

In the Evening

Before I sleep to-night, I want to say a prayer for all the people—known to me and unknown to me—for whom this has been a special day of gladness or of grief, of trouble or of joy.

Bless all the homes in which to-day life has ended or life has begun.

Bless all the homes in which a child has been born, and take special care of the mother and the father and the little baby.

Bless those who have been married to-day, and grant that this may be the beginning for them of many years of loyalty and love.

Bless all homes where there has been joy or heartbreak, where there has been happy news of success or sorrowful news of failure, homes to which someone has brought honour and homes to which someone has brought disgrace.

Be very near to any home in which anyone is tempted to do some disgraceful and dishonourable and evil thing, and lay your hand upon his/her shoulder and restrain them from it.

Be in every home to comfort, to encourage, to guide, to restrain; and grant to them all to feel your presence and to know your love: through Jesus Christ my Lord. AMEN.

Daily Reading

GALATIANS 6: 1-5

Brethren, if a man be overtaken in a fault, ye which are spiritual, restore such a one in the spirit of meekness; considering thyself, lest thou also be tempted. Bear ye one another's burdens, and so fulfil the law of Christ. For if a man thinks himself to be something, when he is nothing, he deceiveth himself. But let every man prove his own work, and then shall he have rejoicing in himself alone, and not in another. For every man shall bear his own burden.

In the Morning

O God, I know that there are certain dangers which are always threatening me.

Keep me from taking people and all that they do for me for granted, and help me to show them how much I value them, and how much I appreciate all that they do for me.

Keep me from allowing myself to become satisfied with less and less, from lowering my standards, from forgetting my ideals as the days go on.

Keep me from taking sin less and less seriously, from allowing myself things which once I would have refused, from accepting as inevitable things which once would have shocked me.

Help me to walk looking unto Jesus, that I may see all things in the light of his life and of his Cross, so that I may strive to be always on the upward way.

This I ask for your love's sake. AMEN.

In the Evening

O God, I thank you for to-day and for your help all through to-day.

There were things which I thought I would never be able to do,
  but with your help I managed to do them.

There were things of which I was frightened as I looked forward to them,
  but with your help I found them not so terrible after all.

I thank you for the pleasure I found in the company of people whom up to now I thought uninteresting, or whom up to now I did not like.

I thank you that life is just as full of unexpected joys as it is of unexpected sorrows.

I thank you for the friends who grow dearer to me every day, and without whom life would never be the same.

I thank you for the people who have given me the generous love which I have done so little to deserve.

Help me to fall asleep to-night counting my blessings.

Hear this my prayer for Jesus' sake. AMEN.

Daily Reading

MICAH 6: 6-8

Wherewith shall I come before the Lord, and bow myself before the high God? shall I come before him with burnt offerings, with calves of a year old? Will the Lord be pleased with thousands of rams, or with ten thousand rivers of oil? shall I give my firstborn for my transgression, the fruit of my body for the sin of my soul? He hath shewed thee, O man, what is good; and what doth the Lord require of thee, but to do justly, and to love mercy, and to walk humbly with thy God?

In the Morning

O God, my Father, I thank you that this morning I am able to rise and to go to my work.

I thank you that I can move and walk, and see and hear, and think with my mind and work with my hands.

As I think of the health which I enjoy, I remember those who are blind and deaf, lame and helpless and bedridden, those who have lost their reason and whose minds are darkened and whose senses are gone.

I remember those who long to work but who are unemployed, whose talents and gifts and skills are wasting in an idleness which they hate.

Help me, O God, to live to-day in such a way that I may show my gratitude for all the gifts and blessings you have given me: through Jesus Christ my Lord. AMEN.

In the Evening

This morning, O God, I thanked you that I was able to rise from sleep and to go out to my work. It is good to go out, but it is still better to come home.

I thank you for keeping me safe to-day on the busy streets, and on my journeys to and from my work.

I thank you for any temptation which you made me able to conquer to-day.

I thank you that I was able to do the work which I was given to do.

I thank you for everyone who helped me and who was kind to me to-day.

I am sorry if I did any of my work badly, or if I hurt or disappointed anyone.

Now guard and keep me while I sleep, and waken me strengthened and refreshed to-morrow morning: through Jesus Christ my Lord. AMEN.

Daily Reading

HEBREWS 4: 12-16

For the word of God is quick, and powerful, and sharper than any two-edged sword, piercing even to the dividing asunder of soul and spirit, and of the joints and marrow, and is a discerner of the thoughts and intents of the heart. Neither is there any creature that is not manifest in his sight: but all things are naked and opened unto the eyes of him with whom we have to do. Seeing then that we have a great high priest, that is passed into the heavens, Jesus the Son of God, let us hold fast our profession. For we have not a high priest which cannot be touched with the feeling of our infirmities; but was in all points tempted like as we are, yet without sin. Let us therefore come boldly unto the throne of grace, that we may obtain mercy, and find grace to help in time of need.

In the Morning

O God, it is you who have given me another day of life. Unless you help me, I know that this day will go all wrong.

Control my tongue.
Keep me from saying things which make trouble, and from involving myself in arguments which only make bad situations worse and which get nowhere.

Control my thoughts.
Shut the door of my mind against all envious and jealous thoughts; shut it against all bitter and resentful thoughts· shut it against all ugly and unclean thoughts.

Help me to live to-day in purity, in humility and in love.

All through to-day grant that no wrong thought may enter my mind and no wrong word come from my mouth : through Jesus Christ my Lord. AMEN.

In the Evening

O God, my Father, to-night in the quiet time I have many people in my mind and in my heart.

Those I love:
Help me never to hurt or to disappoint them, and never to drift apart from them. Bless them and keep them safe.

My friends :
Help me never to be too selfish and too demanding with my friends; never to try to make use of them ;· always to try to do something to enrich their lives, as I wish that they may enrich mine.

The people with whom I work:
> Make me easy to work with. Help me never to make the work of others harder by dodging or shirking the work I ought to be doing. Help me never to be needlessly slow to learn, or impatiently unwilling to show others how to do things, or to help them to do them.

All people in pain, in sadness, in loneliness, in trouble, in disgrace:
> Help those who cannot help themselves, and bless those for whom their fellowmen can do little to comfort or to support.

Bless me, and make me for ever sure of your love and your care.

This I ask for your love's sake. AMEN.

Daily Reading

EXODUS 20: 1-7

And God spake all these words, saying, I am the Lord thy God, which have brought thee out of the land of Egypt, out of the house of bondage. Thou shalt have no other gods before me. Thou shalt not make unto thee any graven image, or any likeness of anything that is in heaven above, or that is in the earth beneath, or that is in the water under the earth: thou shalt not bow down thyself to them, nor serve them: for I the Lord thy God am a jealous God, visiting the iniquity of the fathers upon the children unto the third and fourth generation of them that hate me; and shewing mercy unto thousands of them that love me, and keep my commandments. Thou shalt not take the name of the Lord thy God in vain; for the Lord will not hold him guiltless that taketh his name in vain.

In the Morning

O God, I will meet all kinds of people to-day; help me to help them all.

If I meet any who are sad,
    help me to comfort them, even if I can do no more than
    say a word of sympathy and shake their hand.

If I meet any who are depressed,
    help me to cheer them up, and to send them on their way
    happier because they met me.

If I meet any who are tempted,
    help me to help them to resist temptation by showing them
    an example, or by speaking a gentle word of warning to
    them.

If I meet any who are worried,
    help me to ease their anxiety as far as I can.

If I meet any who are overworked,
    help me to lend them a hand, if I possibly can, even if it
    means extra work for me, and even if I have to go a long
    way out of my way to do so.

If I meet any who are disgruntled and discontented,
    help me to help them to feel that things are not as bad as
    they think they are.

If I meet any who are happy,
    help me to share in their joy, and never to grudge it to
    them.

Make me able to enter into the mind and heart of all whom
I meet to-day, and to bring joy and happiness wherever I go:
through Jesus Christ my Lord. AMEN.

In the Evening

O God, you know how I feel, and you know that to-night I am so tired that I can hardly stay awake to pray.

But, before I go to sleep, I must say thank you for to-day and I must ask your forgiveness for everything in it that was not right.

Help me now to fall asleep thinking about you, and to waken to-morrow to live for you.

This I ask for your love's sake. AMEN.

Daily Reading

EXODUS 20 : 8-17

Remember the sabbath day, to keep it holy. Six days shalt thou labour, and do all thy work; but the seventh day is the sabbath of the Lord thy God : in it thou shalt not do any work, thou, nor thy son, nor thy daughter, thy manservant, nor thy maidservant, nor thy cattle, nor the stranger that is within thy gates; for in six days the Lord made heaven and earth, the sea, and all that in them is, and rested on the seventh day : wherefore the Lord blessed the sabbath day, and hallowed it. Honour thy father and thy mother : that thy days may be long upon the land which the Lord thy God giveth thee. Thou shalt not kill. Thou shalt not commit adultery. Thou shalt not steal. Thou shalt not bear false witness against thy neighbour. Thou shalt not covet thy neighbour's house, thou shalt not covet thy neighbour's wife, nor his manservant, nor his maidservant, nor his ox, nor his ass, nor any thing that is thy neighbour's.

In the Morning

Help me, O God, to-day,
   To shirk no duty that I should face,
   or word that I should speak.

   To avoid no person whom I ought to meet,
   or any decision which I ought to take.

   To postpone no task that I ought to do,
   nor to delay the answer to any request to which I should
      respond.

Help me,
   To do each thing as it comes to me,
   And to do it faithfully, wisely and well.

Keep me alike,
   From delaying the things I ought to do,
   And from rushing into the things, about which I ought to
      think before I act.

All through to-day grant me the wisdom which will keep me
from all mistakes and save me from all regrets: through
Jesus Christ my Lord. AMEN.

In the Evening

Thank you, O God, for making me able to do my work
to-day, and for bringing me back home at evening time.

Thank you for the times to-day when you guided me to do what I ought to do, and when you strengthened me to resist the temptation to do what I ought not to do.

Thank you for anyone you made me able to help to-day, and for anyone to whom I have come closer.

Thank you for those who have helped me to-day, for those who have cheered me when I was depressed, for anyone who went out of his way to help me, for anyone who made me feel that after meeting him life was better than I thought.

Help me to sleep well to-night and to work well to-morrow: through Jesus Christ my Lord. AMEN.

Daily Reading

LUKE 10: 25-28

And, behold, a certain lawyer stood up, and tempted him, saying, Master, what shall I do to inherit eternal life? He said unto him, What is written in the law? how readest thou? And he answering said, Thou shalt love the Lord thy God with all thy heart, and with all thy soul, and with all thy strength, and with all thy mind; and thy neighbour as thyself. And he said unto him, Thou hast answered right: this do, and thou shalt live.

In the Morning

Give me, O God, all through to-day a strong sense of duty,
   so that I will not be able to shirk any task,
   to evade any decision,
   ·or to avoid any responsibility.

Help me to do my duty to myself,
   so that I will never lose my self-respect.

Help me to do my duty to others,
   so that I may be among my fellowmen as one who serves.

Help me to do my duty to you,
   by giving myself to you body, soul and spirit,
   so that you can use me as you wish.

At the same time give me joy in all things, so that duty may
not be a grim and joyless thing, but so that I may do everything as unto you.

This I ask for your love's sake. AMEN.

In the Evening

O God, you are the God of peace, and I am a worrier. Take
away my worry and give me some of your peace.

Help me not to waste my time worrying about things about
   which there is nothing to be done, but help me to accept
   them, and to make the best of them, and to overcome them.

Help me not to worry about things which I myself can mend,
   but to do something about them, even if it means a great
   effort, and even if it means that which is still more difficult

—the confessing of my error and the humbling of my pride.

Help me not to worry about the past. Although I am a sinner, help me to know and to remember that I am a forgiven sinner.

Help me not to worry about the future, but to know that I will never be tried above what I am able to bear.

Help me to-night to sleep in peace, and to waken to-morrow sure that I can face life, and all that life can demand from me, and all that life can do to me.

Hear this my prayer for Jesus' sake. AMEN.

Daily Reading

I CORINTHIANS 13: 1-7

Though I speak with the tongues of men and of angels, and have not charity, I am become as sounding brass, or a tinkling cymbal. And though I have the gift of prophecy, and understand all mysteries, and all knowledge; and though I have all faith, so that I could remove mountains, and have not charity, I am nothing. And though I bestow all my goods to feed the poor, and though I give my body to be burned, and have not charity, it profiteth me nothing. Charity suffereth long, and is kind; charity envieth not; charity vaunteth not itself, is not puffed up, doth not behave itself unseemly, seeketh not her own, is not easily provoked, thinketh no evil; rejoiceth not in iniquity, but rejoiceth in the truth; beareth all things, believeth all things, hopeth all things, endureth all things.

In the Morning

O God, as this day begins for me, I want to remember before you those for whom it will be hard and sad and difficult.

Bless those
Who have no work to do, and for whom the hours will be empty;
Who to-day will have to watch a loved one pass from this life, or lay a dear one to rest;
Who will go out to sadness and come home to loneliness;
Who will be stricken with sudden illness;
Who have to undergo an operation to-day or who must spend it waiting for one;
Who will receive bad news;
To whom this day will bring disappointment and heartbreak.

Grant that all in sorrow, in difficulty, and in hardship may find in you a refuge and strength, and a very present help in their trouble.

This I ask through Jesus Christ my Lord. AMEN.

In the Evening

Take from me to-night, O God,
The worries which would keep me from sleeping;
The tension which would keep me from relaxing;
The envies and the jealousies and the wrong memories, which would make my heart bitter.

Forgive me for the things which I regret and for which I am sorry now; and help me here and now to make up my mind to take the first step to try to put things right to-morrow with anyone whom I have hurt or wronged, or anyone with whom I finished to-day at variance.

Help me to-night to sleep in peace, sure of your love and care surrounding me; and grant that to-morrow I may waken with my mind clear, with my body refreshed, and with my heart at peace with men and with you: through Jesus Christ my Lord. AMEN.

Daily Reading

I CORINTHIANS 13: 8-13

Charity never faileth: but whether there be prophecies, they shall fail; whether there be tongues, they shall cease; whether there be knowledge, it shall vanish away. For we know in part, and we prophesy in part. But when that which is perfect is come, then that which is in part shall be done away. When I was a child, I spake as a child, I understood as a child, I thought as a child: but when I became a man, I put away childish things. For now we see through a glass, darkly; but then face to face: now I know in part; but then shall I know even as also I am known. And now abideth faith, hope, charity, these three; but the greatest of these is charity.

In the Morning

O God, help me to make to-day a perfect day, a day at the end of which I will have nothing to regret.

Help me
    To do my work as well as it can possibly be done;
    To treat everyone with perfect courtesy and kindness;
    To conquer every temptation and to say no to everything that is wrong.

Help me
    Not to annoy anyone else and not to allow myself to become annoyed;
    Not to lose my temper and not to do things which will make others lose theirs;
    Not to do anything that is foolish or thoughtless, cruel or unkind.

Help me
    To be cheerful and kind;
    To be brave and strong;
    To be pure and true.
This I ask for your love's sake. AMEN.

In the Evening

O God, this morning I set out with such good resolutions and with such high intentions to make this a perfect day—but it didn't work out that way.

I am sorry for all the time that I have wasted;
I am sorry for all the people at whom I snapped;
I am sorry that I did silly things, when I wasn't thinking
   what I was doing.

There are so many things which I said and did to-day for
which I am sorry now. I am sorry that I was needlessly
annoying, bad-tempered and unkind.

Help me before I go to sleep to feel that you understand how
difficult it is, and to feel that you have forgiven me. And help
me to do better to-morrow, and never to give up trying:
through Jesus Christ my Lord. AMEN.

Daily Reading

MATTHEW 5: 43-48

Ye have heard that it hath been said, Thou shalt love thy
neighbour, and hate thine enemy. But I say unto you, Love
your enemies, bless them that curse you, do good to them
that hate you, and pray for them which despitefully use you,
and persecute you; that ye may be the children of your Father
which is in heaven: for he maketh his sun to rise on the evil
and on the good, and sendeth rain on the just and on the
unjust. For if ye love them which love you, what reward have
ye? do not even the publicans the same? And if ye salute
your brethren only, what do ye more than others? do not even
the publicans so? Be ye therefore perfect, even as your
Father which is in heaven is perfect.

In the Morning

O God, help me this morning to count my blessings before I start on the day.

I thank you that I have a job to go to and work to do.

I thank you that I have the health and the strength and the skill to do it.

I thank you for my home, and for those who are very near and dear to me.

I thank you for the friends whom I will meet to-day, as I travel, at my work, at my meals, and when my work is done.

I thank you for everything in which I will find pleasure to-day, for work, for games, for books, for pictures, for films, for plays, for music, for dancing, for talks with my friends, and for times with those who are more than friends, and whom I love.

I thank you for Jesus, and for the promise that he is always with me.

Help me in that promise to find my inspiration to goodness, and my protection from sin.

Hear this my prayer for your love's sake. AMEN.

In the Evening

O God, before I sleep to-night, I want to bring to you in my prayer those whom I know who specially need your help.

Bless those in sickness, in illness, and in pain. Give them the cheerfulness, the serenity, the faith which will help them to get well.

Bless those who are sad. Comfort them; take away the ache of their loneliness, and help them to find comfort in going on.

Bless those who are worried. Help them to find the peace of mind which comes from the certainty that they will never be tested beyond what they can bear.

Bless those who are tempted. Give them grace to resist; and give your warning to those who are foolishly playing with fire.

Bless those who are far from home and far from friends, and protect them in body, mind and spirit.

Bless all those who are praying for me to-night as I am praying for them.

Hear this my prayer for your love's sake. AMEN.

Daily Reading

JOHN 13: 31-35

Therefore, when he was gone out, Jesus said, Now is the Son of man glorified, and God is glorified in him. If God be glorified in him, God shall also glorify him in himself, and shall straightway glorify him. Little children, yet a little while I am with you. Ye shall seek me : and as I said unto the Jews, Whither I go, ye cannot come; so now I say to you. A new commandment I give unto you, That ye love one another; as I have loved you, that ye also love one another. By this shall all men know that ye are my disciples, if ye have love one to another.

In the Morning

O God, keep me from the things which are bound to cause trouble.

Keep me from
  The self-will which unreasonably insists on its own way;
  The self-conceit which cannot stand the slightest criticism;
  The touchiness which sees offence where no offence was
    ever intended.

Keep me from
  The tale-bearing tongue;
  From all delight in malicious gossip;
  From repeating that which was said in confidence.

Keep me from
  The eyes which can see nothing but faults;
  The mind which can think only the worst;
  The tongue whose delight it is to criticise.

Help me
  To think with kindness;
  To speak with courtesy;
  To act in love.

Help me to live as one who has been with Jesus.

This I ask for your love's sake. AMEN.

In the Evening

O God, thank you for to-day.

Thank you
   For happy things which came to me quite unexpectedly;
   For things which turned out to be not nearly so bad as I
      expected;
   For difficult things which became quite manageable when I
      faced up to them.

Forgive me for the things I did not do,
   For the letter which is still not answered;
   For the promise which is still not kept;
   For the decision which is still delayed;
   For the habit which is still not given up.

Make me honest enough to see myself as I am, and humble
enough to seek from you the help I need, so that what I
cannot do, your grace may do for me: through Jesus Christ
my Lord. AMEN.

Daily Reading

PROVERBS 3: 13-18

Happy is the man that findeth wisdom, and the man that
getteth understanding. For the merchandise of it is better than
the merchandise of silver, and the gain thereof than fine gold.
She is more precious than rubies; and all the things thou
canst desire are not to be compared unto her. Length of days
is in her right hand; and in her left hand riches and honour.
Her ways are ways of pleasantness, and all her paths are
peace. She is a tree of life to them that lay hold upon her;
and happy is every one that retaineth her.

In the Morning

O God, grant that all through to-day I may never find any request for help a nuisance.

Help me never to find a child a nuisance,
    when he wants me to help him with his lessons,
    or play with him in his games.

Help me never to find a sick person a nuisance,
    if he would like me to spend some time with him,
    or do some service for him.

Help me never to find someone who is old a nuisance,
    even if he is critical of youth,
    settled immovably in his ways,
    demanding of attention.

Help me never to find a nuisance anyone who asks me,
    To show him how to do things;
    To help him in his work;
    To listen to his troubles.

Grant, O God, that I may neither be too immersed in work or too fond of my own pleasure, that I may never be too busy and never too tired, to help those who need help, even if they are the kind of people who get on my nerves and whom I instinctively dislike.

Help me to help, not only when it is pleasant to help, but when help is difficult and when I don't want to give it: through Jesus Christ my Lord. AMEN.

In the Evening

O God, the thing that hurts me most to remember at night is how I hurt others through the day.

Forgive me
>For cruelly and mercilessly criticising others;
>For laughing at people;
>For thinking people fools, and for letting them see that I thought they were.

Forgive me
>For any request that I refused;
>For any sympathy that I did not give;
>For any disloyalty which brought pain to the heart of a friend.

O God, I know that so often I have not treated others as I would wish them to treat me; I have treated them as I would hate to be treated.

Forgive me and help me to be kinder to-morrow: through Jesus Christ my Lord. AMEN.

Daily Reading

PHILIPPIANS 2: 5-11

Let this mind be in you, which was also in Christ Jesus; who, being in the form of God, thought it not robbery to be equal with God: but made himself of no reputation, and took upon him the form of a servant, and was made in the likeness of men; and being found in fashion as a man, he humbled himself, and became obedient unto death, even the death of the cross. Wherefore God also hath highly exalted him, and given him a name which is above every name: that at the name of Jesus every knee should bow, of things in heaven, and things in earth, and things under the earth; and that every tongue should confess that Jesus Christ is Lord, to the glory of God the Father.

IN TIME OF A DISASTER

O God, I remember before you those on whom at this time disaster has come.

Bless those whose dear ones have been killed, and those whose dear ones have lost their lives in seeking to save the lives of others.

Bless those who have lost their homes, and those who have seen all that they toiled for a lifetime to build up lost in an hour.

Help us always to remember those whose job it is to risk their lives to rescue others or to keep them safe—those in the fire-service, in the lifeboat service, in the police service, in the mountain-rescue service, in the medical service.

We will forget this disaster, but we ask you in your love always to remember those who will never forget because life for them can never be the same again.

This we ask for your love's sake. AMEN.

AT THE TIME OF A
HOLIDAY TRAGEDY

O God, Father of all comfort and God of all grace,

Bless those for whom the joy of holiday time has turned to tragedy;

Those who have lost dear ones in accidents on the roads, on the beaches and at sea, in the hills, on the railways, in the air, by the sudden and unexpected coming of death into their family circle.

Help us to remember that there is always someone who is sad, that never morning wore to evening but some heart did break, and comfort those for whom happy days in the sunshine turned suddenly to the midnight of a broken heart.

This I ask for your love's sake. AMEN

FOR A HAPPY ANNIVERSARY

O God, to-day I am happy as I look back and remember.

I thank you for that day . . . years ago which was the beginning of joy for me.

I thank you for the happy years you have given to me in my home, at my work, within my Church.

I thank you for all the friends and the comrades and the loved ones with whom throughout the years my life has been intertwined.

This day, as you have commanded me, I remember all the way by which you have brought me to this present hour, and I thank you for it.

Hear this my thanksgiving through Jesus Christ my Lord. AMEN.

FOR A SAD ANNIVERSARY

O God, to-day brings me memories that are sad.

Sometimes in the busy world and at my work I can forget. But you have given us hearts which are so vulnerable, and the sight of a place, a photograph, a tune, the sound of a word, and above all a day like this sets my heart throbbing with pain again, and I feel again the blank in life which nothing can fill.

Help me not to sorrow overmuch as those who have no hope. Help me still to face life with steady eyes, remembering that the one I loved is not gone for ever, but that another has been added to the unseen cloud of witnesses who compass me about.

And bring quickly the time when the memories which make me cry will be the memories which make me smile : through Jesus Christ my Lord. AMEN.

FOR A WEDDING ANNIVERSARY

O God, I thank you that you have given us another year of life together.

I thank you
  For the love which grows more precious and for the bonds
    which grow more close each day.

I thank you
  For the happiness we have known together;
  For the sorrows we have faced together;
  For all the experiences of sunshine and of shadow through
    which we have come to to-day.

I ask your forgiveness
  For any disloyalty on my part;
  For any times when I was difficult to live with;
  For any selfishness and inconsiderateness;
  For any lack of sympathy and of understanding;
  For anything which spoiled even for a moment the perfect
    relationship which marriage should be.

Spare us to each other to go on walking the way of life together, and grant that for us it may be true that the best is yet to be : through Jesus Christ my Lord. AMEN.

A BIRTHDAY PRAYER

O God, I thank you for giving me another year of life.

I thank you for all the people who have remembered me to-day, and who have sent me cards, and letters, and good wishes, and presents.

I thank you for everything which I have been enabled by you to do and to be in the past year.

I thank you for all the experiences of the past year;
For times of success which will always be happy memories;
For times of failure which reminded me of my own weakness and of my need of you;
For times of joy when the sun was shining;
For times of sorrow which drove me to you.

Forgive me
For the hours I have wasted;
For the chances I failed to take;
For the opportunities I missed in the past year.

Forgive me that I have not made of life all that I might have made of it and could have made of it; and help me in the days which lie ahead to make this the best year yet, and in it to bring credit to myself, happiness to my loved ones, and joy to you.

This I ask for Jesus' sake. AMEN.

Thank you, O God, for the success which you have given me to-day.

Help me not to rest on my oars because I achieved something, but to work still harder, to aim still higher, to do still better.

Keep me from becoming conceited. Help me always to think, not of what I have done, but of what I still must do; not of the few things in which I have succeeded, but of the many things in which I have failed.

Help me to be happy in the joy of achievement, but save me from a boastful and a foolish pride.

This I ask for Jesus' sake. AMEN.

O God, you know how badly I have failed in the task which I attempted, and which was given me to do, and in which I so much wanted to do well.

Don't let me become too depressed and discouraged; help me to have the determination to try again and to work still harder.

Don't let me try to put the blame on everyone and on everything except myself.

Don't let me be resentful and bitter about this failure; but help me to accept both success and failure with a good grace.

Don't let me be envious and jealous of those who have succeeded where I have failed.

Don't ever let me talk about giving up and giving in; but help me to refuse to be beaten.

Help me to learn the lesson which you want me to learn even from this failure; help me to begin again, and not to make the same mistakes again.

Maybe it is hardest of all to meet the eyes of those who are disappointed in me. Help me even yet to show them that I deserve their trust and to let them see what I can do.

This I ask for your love's sake. AMEN.

FOR ONE WHO IS TIRED

O God, somehow nowadays I am always tired. I go to sleep tired and I get up still tired.

Things take longer than they used to take, and I get behind with my work, and with the things I ought to do.

I come home tired, and that makes me cross and bad-tempered and irritable and impatient with my own family and my own people.

Everything has become an effort and a labour.

O God, help me to keep going, and help me to find something of the rest which you alone can give. Refresh me with your presence, and give me back the joy of living and the thrill of working: through Jesus Christ my Lord. AMEN.

FOR ONE WHO IS TEMPTED

O God, there are things about which I can't talk to anyone except to you. There are things in me about which no one knows except myself and you.

The things which I should not even want fascinate me. The thoughts which I should never allow into my mind, I cannot keep out.

So far I have resisted the wrong things, but I know my own weakness, and I am afraid of myself.

O God, come to me with your cleansing power, and make me able to overcome evil and to do the right.

I ask even more—fill me with such a love of you that I will not even want to sin any more.

This I ask for Jesus' sake. AMEN.

FOR ONE WHO HAS FALLEN
TO TEMPTATION

O God, I know that there is nothing which I can hide from you. I can hide my failure and my shame from others, but I cannot hide them from you. You know what I have done, and you know how sorry I am for it.

I am sorry more than anything else for the way in which I have hurt and disappointed and failed those who hoped in me, and believed in me, and love me.

I have come to you to ask for your forgiveness, to ask for strength and grace and courage to face up to things, to try even yet to redeem myself.

Forgive me. Keep me from doing the same wrong thing again. Help me to live from now on in that purity and that honesty and that goodness which you alone can give, and which you alone can preserve.

Hear this my prayer for your love's sake. AMEN.

FOR ONE WHO IS SAD

O God, I come to you for comfort.

You know how lonely I am without . . . There are so many things which keep reminding me of . . . , and of all that I have lost.

O God, keep me from living too much in the past. Keep me from living too much with memories and too little with hopes.

Keep me from being too sorry for myself. Help me to remember that I am going through what many another has gone through. Help me not to sorrow as those who have no hope.

Help me to find comfort in my work, and, because I have gone through sorrow myself, help me to help others who are in trouble. Help me to keep trying to face life with gallantry, until I meet again the loved one whom I have lost awhile.

This I ask for your love's sake. AMEN.

FOR ONE WHOSE NERVES
HAVE BROKEN DOWN

O God, I have come to the stage when I cannot face life any longer.

I get so tense that I cannot relax. Always at the back of my mind there is the fear that I will get worse than I am now.

I know that nothing can help me, unless I help myself. I cannot help myself, and so, because things have got beyond me, I come to you.

Help me to feel that you know, that you understand, and that you care.

I used to love my work, but now I am frightened of it. I used to love life, but now I am afraid of it.

Give me the peace which comes from stopping struggling and from leaving things to you. Help me really to cast myself and my burden on you. Give me the courage to face my life, myself, my work, and the world again. Help me to win this battle which I know that by myself I can only lose.

Hear this my prayer, for your love's sake. AMEN.

FOR ONE WHO IS SELFISH

O God, in my heart of hearts, when I stop and think, I know that I am selfish.

I always want things done for me. I always want my own way. I demand from others far more than I am prepared to give. If I am honest, I have got to admit that I try to make use of people. I never think of the trouble that I give to others. I know that I am thoughtless, and I know that I am often careless of the feelings of others, that I often hurt them because I am thinking of myself and of no one else. I know that I am so often ungrateful, that I forget how much I owe to others, and that I very seldom make any attempt to repay it.

O God, make me aware, not just at odd moments, but all the time, how ugly this selfishness is. Fix before my eyes the example and the Cross of my Lord, who, though he was rich, yet for my sake became poor. Help me to dethrone self, and to enthrone him within my heart, so that I may learn from him to love others and not myself.

This I ask for your love's sake. AMEN.

FOR ONE WHO IS PROUD

O God, I know that my besetting sin is pride.

So often I find myself looking down on others, and even despising them. I find myself thinking of my own cleverness, and of my own triumphs and achievements. I find myself thinking that I am sensible, and that other people are fools.

O God, take away my pride and my self-conceit.

Help me not to compare myself with other people, but to compare myself with Jesus, so that, when I set myself in the light of his goodness and of his beauty, I may never again be satisfied with myself. Help me to set myself in the light of his holiness, so I may see how unworthy, how inadequate, how ignorant I am.

And, when shame replaces pride, give me your grace, so that through it I may find in you the things I know I need and have not got.

Hear this my prayer, for your love's sake. AMEN.

FOR ONE WITH A
QUICK TEMPER

O God, I know that my temper is far too quick.

I know only too well how liable I am to flare up, and to say things for which afterwards I am heartily sorry.

I know only too well that sometimes in anger I do things which in my calmer moments I would never have done.

I know that my temper upsets things at home; that it makes me difficult to work with; that it makes me lose my friends; that far too often it makes me a cause and source of trouble.

O God, help me. Help me to think before I speak. When I feel that I am going to blaze out, help me to keep quiet just for a moment or two, until I get a grip of myself again. Help me to remember that you are listening to everything I say, and seeing everything I do.

O God, control me and my temper too.

This I ask for your love's sake. AMEN.

FOR SOMEONE WHO
PUTS THINGS OFF

O God, I know how apt I am to put things off.

Sometimes it is because I am too lazy to do them. Sometimes it is just because I am afraid to do them. Sometimes it is because I just can't make up my mind, and I shilly-shally, and can't make a decision. Sometimes it is because I say to myself that to-morrow will be time enough.

I know that I have got into this bad habit, and I know that it causes trouble for myself and for other people, and I am only too well aware that because of it things that ought to have been done have never been done—and some of them can never be done at all now.

O God, help me to do better.

Help me to remember that for all I know to-morrow may never come.

Give me resolution to make up my mind, and strength and courage to act on my decision.

Help me never to leave until to-morrow what I ought to do to-day; and help me within each day to do the tasks and to make the decisions which the day demands.

Hear this my prayer for your love's sake. AMEN.

FOR ONE WHO IS IN
TOO BIG A HURRY

O God, I know that I am in far too big a hurry.

I dash at things with far too little preparation, and without thinking of the consequences of them. Far too often I speak and act without thinking. Far too often I start something without counting the cost.

I am far too impatient both with things and with people. I have never learned to wait. I try to do things as quickly as I can and not as well as I can. My life is full of sudden enthusiasms which blaze up and just as quickly die down.

The result of all this is that my life is full of things I began and never finished, and took up and never continued, and which have to be done all over again because they were done in far too big a hurry. My frantic efforts to save time just waste time in the end.

Help me to take a grip of myself. Help me to take time to think. Give me patience to wait and perseverance to continue. Help me to think of how slowly and patiently you work, and to remember that it is better to do things well than to do them quickly.

Hear this my prayer for your love's sake. AMEN.

FOR CONTENTMENT

O God, keep me from grumbling.

I am quite well aware—from experience—that there is no one harder to put up with than someone who is always complaining. Don't let me become like that. Don't let me have discontentment written all over my face, and the whine of the east wind for ever in my voice.

If I can't get my own way,
don't let me sulk about it.

If I can't get what I want,
help me to make the best of what I can get, and of what I have.

Don't let me become one of these people who take offence far too easily, and who go off in the huff, even when nothing unpleasant was ever intended.

Help me all day every day
to look on the bright side of things,
and to see the best in people.

And help me to live in the certainty that you are working all things together for good, if I have only the trust to accept them, and the patience to wait for your purposes to work out.

This I ask for your love's sake. AMEN.

THAT I MAY NOT WASTE
THE PRECIOUS THINGS
OF LIFE

O God,
Help me not to waste my time. Don't let me always be in a hurry and a fuss, but help me to go on quietly and without haste, filling every minute with the work which is given me to do.

Help me not to waste my strength. Help me to see quite clearly the things which matter and the things which don't matter. Give me a sense of proportion that I may not get all hot and bothered about things which are of no importance, and so make myself too tired and exhausted to do the things which really matter.

Help me not to waste my money. Don't let me be mean and miserly, but help me to spend wisely and to give generously, and to try to use everything I have remembering that it belongs, not to me, but to you.

Above all, help me not to waste my life. Help me to use the talents you have given me; to seize the opportunities you are sending to me, so that some day you may be able to say to me: Well done!

You are the Lord and Master of all good life; hear this my prayer and help me to live well: through Jesus Christ my Lord. AMEN.

O God, you have given us your own day to worship and to rest. Bless all those who to-morrow will preach and proclaim your word.

Give them a message from you to their people. Grant that on their lips the old themes may become new, and the old story as vivid as if it had never been told before.

Give them such a love of truth that they will think of nothing but to speak it; but give them also such a love and care for their people that they will speak the truth in sympathy and in love.

Give them, as they speak,
A word of comfort
for the sad in heart;

A word of certainty and of light
for the seeking and the searching and the doubting mind;

A word of strength
for those who are wrestling with temptation;

A word of grace
for those who are very conscious of their sin.

Bless all who to-morrow will worship in your house.

Grant that their time of worship may not be a nuisance which must be endured, or a respectable convention which must be observed. Grant that they may come in joy, in faith, and in expectation; and make them very sure that none will be sent empty away.

Bless all Church members who will not worship in your house to-morrow.

If they are held at home by sickness or by the care of the sick, by the care of children and of household things, by weakness or by age, because they must work even on Sunday, or because they were too sad to come, make them to know that you and we remember them. If they stayed away because they did not wish to come, make them to remember their vows and to worship as they ought.

Bless those to whom the Church is nothing, and who will never even think of coming.

If they have forgotten you, we know that you have not forgotten them; and help us to bring your lost children back into the family of the Church.

Hear this my prayer through Jesus Christ my Lord. AMEN.

PRAYERS BEFORE GOING
TO CHURCH

O God, bring me to your Church in the right spirit to-day.

Grant that in my heart there may be no bitterness to anyone, and help me to remember that I cannot be at one with you, if I am not at one with my fellowmen.

Take from me the critical and fault-finding spirit, so that I may really and truly go to Church only to worship.

Take from me the selfish and the self-centred spirit, so that I may think, not only of what I am going to get out of this service, but also of what I am going to give and to bring to it.

Bless my minister. Give him a message for his people to-day, and uphold and support him in the high task you have given him to do.

Grant that in Church to-day I may seek for nothing but to hear your truth and to see Jesus.

This I ask for your love's sake. AMEN.

O God, help me this morning to worship you in spirit and in truth.

Make me willing to listen to the truth, even if the truth hurts and condemns me.

Keep my thoughts from wandering, and help me to concentrate on listening to you.

Help me not only to listen to the prayers, and not only to repeat them, but really to share in them.

Put out of my heart every bitter and unforgiving thought which would be a barrier between me and you. Help me to remember that I cannot have your friendship, if I am out of friendship with my fellowmen.

Help me to go to Church to-day with no other purpose than to listen to your word to me. Take from me the critical spirit and give me the mind and heart which are ready and open to receive.

Bless the preacher; and give him a message this morning for his waiting people, and give him strength and courage, grace and winsomeness to deliver it. Grant that this morning the whole congregation may be saying: Sir, we would see Jesus.

This I ask for your love's sake. AMEN.

A PRAYER AFTER CHURCH

O God, don't let me forget everything that I heard and felt in Church to-day.

Don't let me think that any word of warning and rebuke was meant for other people but not for me.

Don't let me forget that moment when I really did feel that you were near and close to me.

Don't let me forget the sorrow and the regret and the repentance which in that moment I really did feel for the wrong things in life; and don't let me forget the way in which I did feel that I must, with your help, be better.

Don't let the fact that to-day I met Jesus and listened to your word all go for nothing.

This I ask for your love's sake. AMEN.

Prepare me in mind and heart, O God, to listen to and to receive what your word has to say to me.

Bind me in loving fellowship with this group of people with whom I study, so that we may all be able to talk with freedom, knowing that no one will misunderstand, and no one will take offence.

Guard me from the prejudices which would blind me to the truth. Keep me from reading into your word what I want to hear, and rather help me humbly to listen to what you want to say to me.

Help me to bring to the study of your word all the help that the saints and the scholars of the past and the present can give to me to help me to understand it better; and grant that I may fearlessly follow the truth wherever it may lead me.

And then, when I have learned from your word what you want me to do, give me grace and strength to go out and to do it : through Jesus Christ my Lord. AMEN.

A CHURCH OFFICE-BEARER'S PRAYER

O God, to whom the Church belongs, thank you for giving me a special task and a special place within it.

Help me never to think of my office in the Church as a position of honour; help me always to think of it as an opportunity of service. Help me never to think of it as a privilege without thinking of it as a responsibility. Help me never to think of it as an opportunity to rule others; help me always to think of it as an obligation to serve others. So grant that my position may never make me proud, but that it may always keep me humble.

Help me never to make trouble, but always to make peace. So help me always to speak the truth, but always to speak it in love.

Help me never to stand on the letter of the law; never to be concerned with my own rights, my own place, my own importance. Help me to remember that he who would be chief must be the servant of all.

Make me faithful in my duty to the members of this congregation, and help me always to uphold the hands of my minister in sympathy and in prayer.

And out in the world at my day's work and in my pleasure make me a good advertisement for the Church which it is my honour to serve: through Jesus Christ my Lord. AMEN.

A CHOIR MEMBER'S
AND AN ORGANIST'S
PRAYER

Thank you, O God, for giving me the privilege of leading the praise of your people in your house to-day.

Help me always to remember that this is not an opportunity to show my talents but to serve you and your people in your house. So banish from my heart every thought of self and pride, and help me to sing and to make music only because I truly love you with my whole heart.

Help me to remember that there are those whose hearts can be reached and touched by music even more than by speech, and so help me to remember that I too have my ministry and I too to-day can bring someone to you.

This I ask for Jesus' sake. AMEN.

A SUNDAY SCHOOL TEACHER'S PRAYER

Lord Jesus, I remember that you said : Let the little children come to me, and never try to stop them. I thank you that you have honoured me by giving me the task of bringing boys and girls to you.

Help me to do this great work as it ought to be done.

Grant that I may never meet these boys and girls unprepared. Help me to remember that, if I am teaching, I must be always learning. Help me to remember that, if I am a teacher, I must never stop being a scholar.

Grant that I may wisely and lovingly combine the discipline which will make the boys and girls respect me, and the kindness which will make them love me. Help me never to lose patience and never to lose my temper, however inattentive and troublesome they may be. Help me never to stop loving them. And help me throughout the weeks to build up a relationship with them in which they will come and ask me about anything which is worrying them, sure that I will always be ready to listen to them and always ready to understand and to sympathise.

Grant that I may always respect them and be strictly honest with them, and that I may never to save bother tell them something which they will afterwards have to unlearn.

Help me
    To teach them to think;
    To teach them to live;
    To teach them to love.

And at all times help me to teach more by what I am than by what I say.

This I ask for your love's sake. AMEN.

A BIBLE CLASS LEADER'S
PRAYER

O God, you have given me a very difficult job to do within your Church.

Help me never to face these young people unprepared.

Help me to be absolutely honest with them. Help me never to dodge their questions, and never to evade their problems.

Help me to try to understand them before I criticise them. Keep me from the foolishness of looking for old heads on young shoulders, and help me to remember that the ways of one generation are not the ways of another, and that things are different since I was their age.

Help me never to laugh at them, and never to lose patience with them. Help me to be wise enough to know when they need control and discipline, and when it is better to let them have their own way.

Help me to help them to think, to worship and to pray.

Help me to remember that, whether I like it or not, and whether I know it or not, they will judge the Church by me, and that this is the grave responsibility that is laid upon me.

Even if I see no result, help me not to be discouraged. Help me to remember that it takes a long time for a seed to become a tree, and help me to sow the seed and to leave its growth to you.

Grant that what I am may never undo all that I say. You have given me this part of your work to do—help me to do it well.

This I ask for your love's sake. AMEN.

A PARSON'S PRAYER

Lord Jesus, you have very specially called me to be a fellow-worker with you.

Make me diligent in my preparation to preach, determined never to offer to you or to my people that which cost me nothing.

Make me faithful in my visitation, a shepherd who bears each one of his flock upon his heart.

Make me constant in prayer, so that I may never go out to meet men until I have met you.

Help me to meet opposition, obstruction, misunderstanding, misrepresentation with your gentleness, your love, and your forgiveness.

Help me never to lose faith and hope even when nothing seems to be happening, but help me to be content to sow the good seed and to leave the increase to you.

Help me never to lose my temper, never to speak in irritation, never to be on terms of enmity with any man.

Give me firmness and resolution to stand for what I believe to be right, yet give me sympathy and tolerance to understand the point of view of others.

Help me never to make anyone feel a nuisance when he comes to see me, and help me to suffer even fools gladly.

Make me like you, among my fellowmen as one who serves.

This I ask for your love's sake. AMEN.

O God, bless all those who have gone out to bring the message of the gospel to other lands.

I remember before you
> Those who have to endure hardship and discomfort;
> Those who have to face peril and danger;
> Those who have had to leave their families and their children behind while they went out to other lands;
> Those who have to struggle with a new language and with new ways of thought;
> Those whose health has broken down under the strain, and who have had to come home, not knowing whether they will ever be fit for their task again;
> Those who have to face constant discouragement in a situation in which no progress ever seems to be made.

Especially bless those who work in countries where new nations are being born, and where there is strife and trouble and bitterness in the birth-pangs of the new age.

Bless those who preach in the villages and the towns and the cities; those who teach in the schools and the colleges; those who work in the hospitals and among the sick; those who have laid their gifts of craftsmanship or administration on the altar of missionary service.

Help us at home never to forget them and always to pray for them. And help us to give generously of our money to their work so that it may go where we ourselves cannot go.

And bring quickly the day when the knowledge of you will cover the earth as the waters cover the sea: through Jesus Christ my Lord. AMEN.

A PRAYER
FOR THOSE WHO ARE
NEWLY MARRIED

O God, we two want to begin our life together with you, and we want always to continue it with you.

Help us never to hurt and never to grieve one another.

Help us to share all our work, all our hopes, all our dreams, all our successes and all our failures, all our sorrows and all our joys. Help us to have no secrets from one another, so that we may be truly one.

Keep us always true to one another, and grant that all the years ahead may draw us ever closer to one another. Grant that nothing may ever come between us, and nothing may ever make us drift apart.

And, as we live with one another, help us to live with you, so that our love may grow perfect in your love, for you are the God whose name is love.

This we ask for your love's sake. AMEN.

A MOTHER'S PRAYER

O God, help me always to remember that you have given to me the most important task in the world, the task of making a home.

Help me to remember this when I am tired of making beds, and washing clothes, and cooking meals, and cleaning floors, and mending clothes, and standing in shops. Help me to remember it when I am physically tired in body, and when I am weary in mind with the same things which have to be done again and again, day in and day out.

Help me never to be irritable, never to be impatient, never to be cross. Keep me always sweet. Help me to remember how much my husband and my children need me, and help me not to get annoyed when they take me for granted, and when they never seem to think of the extra work they sometimes cause me.

Help me to make this home such that the family will always be eager to come back to it, and such that, when the children grow up and go out to their own homes, they will have nothing but happy memories of the home from which they have come.

This I ask for your love's sake. AMEN.

A FATHER'S PRAYER

O God, help me to be true to the great privilege and the great responsibility which you have given to me.

Help me to be an example and a friend to my children, and a real partner to my wife.

Don't let me get so busy with work and with outside things that I am almost a stranger in my own home, and that I take no interest in household things.

Don't let me take all that is done for me for granted, and help me to keep love alive within the home.

Keep me from habits which make the work of the house harder, and from ways which irritate and annoy, or which get on the nerves of those who live with me.

Give me health and strength and work to do, to earn a living for those who depend on me and whom I love so much; but help me to remember that love is always more important than money.

O God, you have given me the name of father; you have given me your own name; help me to be true to it.

This I ask for your love's sake. AMEN.

A SON'S OR A DAUGHTER'S PRAYER

Thank you, O God, for the home and for the parents you have given me.

Thank you for

All the loving care which I received when I was a child and when I could not care for myself;

All that was provided for me—food and clothes and shelter —in the years before I could earn my own living and support myself;

All the opportunities of education and of learning which my parents gave to me;

All the security I have enjoyed, the door of home always open, the sympathy and the love when I was hurt or discouraged or depressed.

Thank you for all the loving care with which I have been surrounded ever since I was born.

Forgive me, if I have done anything to hurt or to grieve my parents, and, if, as I have grown older, I have drifted away from them until we are almost strangers.

or,

Thank you, if the passing of the years has made me understand my parents better, and has made me love them more, and has drawn me closer and closer to them.

Forgive me, if I have taken everything for granted, if sometimes I just made use of my home, if I took everything and gave nothing.

Forgive me, if sometimes I have been difficult to live with, irritable, rebellious, disobedient, uncommunicative, impatient of advice, angry at restraint.

Help me at least to try to do something to show my gratitude, and to try to repay the debt I owe, even if it never can be fully repaid.

Help me so to value my home, so to love my parents, so to show them that I love them, that some day, when they are gone and I look back, I may have nothing to regret.

Hear this my prayer for Jesus' sake. AMEN.

Lord Jesus, when you lived and worked and talked amongst men in Palestine, they called you Teacher.

Help me to remember the greatness of the work which has been given to me to do.

Help me always to remember that I work with the most precious material in the world, the mind of a child. Help me always to remember that I am making marks upon that mind which time will never rub out.

Give me patience with those who are slow to learn, and even with those who refuse to learn.

When I have to exercise discipline, help me to do so in sternness and yet in love. Keep me from the sarcastic and the biting tongue, and help me always to encourage and never to discourage those who are doing their best, even if that best is not very good.

Help me to help these children, not only to store things in their memories, but to be able to use their minds, and to think for themselves.

And amidst all the worries and the irritations and the frustrations of my job, help me to remember that the future of the nation and of the world is in my hands.

This I ask for your love's sake. AMEN.

A DOCTOR'S PRAYER

Lord Jesus, when you were on earth, you healed all those who had need of healing.

Help me always to remember that you have honoured me by giving me the task of continuing your healing work.

Give me skill in my mind, gentleness on my hands, and sympathy in my heart.

Help me always to remember that often when people come to me, they are frightened and nervous, and help me always to try to bring to them, not only healing for their bodies, but also calm to their minds.

Make me patient yet firm with the foolish malingerer who wastes my time.

When I must tell people that there is nothing that human skill or hands can do for them, give me a wise gentleness to break the news to them.

Help me never to lose the thrill of bringing new life into the world, and never to become callous to the pathos of the parting of death.

Give me something of your skill to heal men's diseases, to ease men's pains, and to bring peace to men's troubled minds.

This I ask for your love's sake. AMEN.

A PRAYER
FOR THOSE WHO SERVE
THE COMMUNITY

*in Town and District Councils, and in Parliament,
in Trades Unions, and in all Public Service*

O God, grant that in all the public work which has been given to me to do my only motive may be to serve my fellow-men, and my only master may be my conscience.

Help me to set loyalty to the right things above all loyalty to party or to class.

Grant that the importance of my work may never make me full of my own self-importance, but rather that it may make me humbly eager to serve and to help the people whom I represent.

Give me wisdom in my mind, clearness in my thinking, truth in my speaking, and always love in my heart, so that I may try always to unite people and never to divide them.

Help me always to set the interests of the community above those of the party; the interest of the nation above the interest of the community; and faithfulness to you above everything else.

So grant that at the end of the day I may win the approval of my own conscience, the respect of men, and your Well done! This I ask for the sake of Jesus who was among his fellowmen as one who served. AMEN.

A PRAYER FOR THOSE
IN AUTHORITY

for Masters, Employers, Managers, Foremen, Directors

O God, you have given me the great responsibility of being in authority over my fellowmen.

Help me always to act fairly and justly; but to justice help me always to add mercy and sympathy. Help me to know when to enforce discipline and when to relax it. Help me never to be guilty of prejudice against any man or favouritism for any man.

Help me to remember that people are always more important than things, and that men are always more important than machines.

Keep me from exercising my authority in harshness or in tyranny, and keep me also from being afraid to exercise it at all, and help me by my presence and my example to make myself and those who work under me one united band of brothers.

Help me to remember that, though I am called master, I too have a Master, even Jesus Christ.

Hear this my prayer for your love's sake. AMEN.

A SCHOLAR'S PRAYER

O God, you are the source and the giver of all wisdom and of all truth. I lay no claim to the name of scholar, but life has set me in this University/College/School, where I must learn and where I must teach.

Give me diligence, perseverance, accuracy in my study, and help me to seek for truth as blind men long for light.

Give me clarity, sympathy, enthusiasm in my teaching, and grant that I may ever seek to open the minds of those whom I teach to beauty and to truth. And grant that I may never wish those whom I teach to think as I think, but that I may ever seek to teach them to think for themselves.

Grant that my life within this place of learning may not separate and isolate me from the life and work of the world of business and of trade and of industry and of commerce.

Grant that at the end of the day I may have taken a little further the torch of knowledge and of truth which was handed on to me.

This I ask for your love's sake and for your truth's sake. AMEN.

A FARMER'S OR
A GARDENER'S PRAYER

O God, I thank you for the gifts which the garden, the fields and the orchards bring to us.

I thank you for the green of the grass and the colours of the flowers, and for all the loveliness of nature which is more beautiful than the robes of kings. I thank you for all the growing things which bring food and health to men.

I thank you for the sleep of the winter, the rebirth of the spring, the golden glory of the summer, for the harvest of the autumn.

Grant that the mysterious way in which growth goes on, silently and unseen, night and day, may always make me think of you, the giver of it all.

I thank you that you gave to me the love of the soil and of all growing things, and the gift of green fingers which know nature's ways and secrets.

Help me in nature's life to see you who are the giver of all life, and to catch a glimpse of the endless life which death can never destroy: through Jesus Christ my Lord. AMEN.

O God, I thank you for your gift to men of music.
I thank you

For the music which tells of the sorrows of the human
heart, and which can also soothe them;

For the music which expresses human joy;

For the music which thrills and challenges the spirit of
man;

For the music which says things which words are powerless
to say.

I thank you that you gave me the ability to enjoy music and to
understand it. I thank you for the ability to create it. I
thank you alike for the music which makes the feet of men
dance and for the music which makes the hearts of men
pray.

Help me to worship and to serve you in your gift of music,
and grant that I may always be ready to use this gift of mine
for your service and for the joy of men: through Jesus Christ
my Lord. AMEN.

A PRAYER FOR
SHOP ASSISTANTS

and for all who serve the Public

Lord Jesus, you have given me the task of serving the public —and it isn't always easy.

Help me to be patient with the time-wasting.

Help me to be courteous to the discourteous.

Help me to be forbearing to the unreasonable.

Help me to be always cheerful, always obliging, always willing to go the extra mile in service.

Make me such that people will go away happier and smiling because I served them to-day.

Hear this my prayer for your love's sake. AMEN.

AN OFFICE-WORKER'S PRAYER

O God, my work is with the typewriter and the comptometer and the ledger and the accounts and the invoices and things like that.

It isn't work that is much in the limelight or that people see very much of. I am just like a very small cog in a very big machine. But help me to remember that no machine can run well unless even the smallest part of it is doing its job.

So help me to be careful and punctual in my work. Help me to be interested in my work and to take a pride in it. Keep me from making careless mistakes which hold things up and which mean that things have to be done over again and which waste everyone's time. Help me to be willing and easy to work with.

And help me always to be courteous and cheerful so that this office will be a happier place, because I work in it: through Jesus Christ my Lord. AMEN.

Lord Jesus, help me to love my job, and help me to feel that I am really doing your work, and really helping you, when I look after people who are sick.

Help me at all times to have
    Patience with the unreasonable, the querulous and the irritating;
    Sympathy with the frightened and the nervous;
    And never let me neglect those who are quiet and uncomplaining.

When people telephone or come to ask how their friends or loved ones are getting on, help me to remember how worried and anxious they are, and to do my best to help them.
Give me a steady nerve when difficult things have to be done. Make me very attentive to orders and instructions and very obedient in carrying them out; and in an emergency make me able to think for myself and to come quickly to a decision.

    Give me skill; but give me gentleness.
    Give me efficiency; but make me kind.
    Make me firm; but make me understanding too.

Help me to study with diligence and to work with willingness; and help me to love my work and to love the people whom it is my work to help.

This I ask for your love's sake. AMEN.

A PRAYER
FOR THOSE WHO ADMINISTER
THE LAW

O God, I know that it is from you that men have learned what goodness and justice are.

Give me a mind that is fair and impartial, and give me the power to judge and to decide with wisdom and with equity. Grant that nothing may ever make me pervert the course of justice, neither the promise of reward nor the threat of vengeance. Grant that I may never be influenced either by the fear or the favour of men.

Make me to know that there are times when mercy is greater than justice, and when love is better than law.

Help me to help others rather to settle their disputes and differences in peace and friendship than to pursue them in bitterness and contention; and make me, not only an expert in the law, but also a wise counsellor to those who come to me for help and for advice: through Jesus Christ my Lord. AMEN.

A POLICEMAN'S PRAYER

O God, you have given me the task of maintaining law and order in this community. It is a much more dangerous and frustrating task than once it was.

Give me the courage and the resolution at all times to do my duty, and give me such a love and respect for justice that neither promise nor threat will ever make me depart from it.

Help me in a real sense to be the Guardian and the Friend of the whole community, a friend to the children, an example to youth, a counsellor and adviser to all good citizens.

Give me the skill and the wisdom and the strength I need to capture the evil-doer and to keep him from his misdeeds. And give me at all times wisdom to know when to enforce and when to relax the letter of the law.

Help me to be a personal example of the honesty, the goodness, the justice which it is my duty to maintain; and help me to win the authority which comes from respect: through Jesus Christ my Lord. AMEN.

A PRAYER FOR THOSE
IN THE FIRE SERVICE AND
THE LIFE-BOAT SERVICE

*and for all those
whose task it is to rescue others*

O God, you have given to me the task of rescuing those who are in trouble and in danger. Help me to find pride and pleasure in the thought that there is no greater task than the task of saving others.

Sometimes I have to risk my own life in seeking to save the life and the property of others. When I think of the perils which I must face, and when I remember those who gave their lives in facing them, help me to remember that Jesus said: Greater love hath no man than this, that a man lay down his life for his friends.

Others may have better-paid jobs, and jobs which are safer and in which the hours and the work are easier, but no one has a bigger and a more important job than I have.

Lord Jesus, you are the Saviour of the world; help, strengthen and protect me that in my own way and in my own sphere I too may be ready to risk all to save others.

This I ask for your love's sake. AMEN.

A CIVIL SERVANT'S PRAYER

O God, you have given me a share in the administration of this country. I don't hit the headlines in the newspapers; people don't know my name as they know the names of the famous politicians, and members of Parliament, and members of the government. But help me always to have the great satisfaction of knowing that they would be helpless without the ordinary routine work which I have to do, and that without it the life of the country would come to a stop. So give me joy and pride in my work, even if it is unseen.

Help me to be efficient, but not soulless.

Help me always to remember that, although I usually never see them, I am dealing with real flesh and blood people with hearts that can be hurt and minds which can be bewildered, and not with names on a schedule or numbers on a card index.

Give me courtesy, even when I have to enforce regulations which dishonest people are trying to dodge.

In all my work help me to remember that I am a human being dealing with human beings.

This I ask for your love's sake. AMEN.

A PRAYER FOR
A WELFARE WORKER OR
A SOCIAL WORKER

O God, I sometimes think that I have the hardest job of all, because what I am really trying to do is to make bad people good and to make foolish people wise—and it is a hard job.

Help me
  Never to lose patience;
  Never to abandon hope;
  Never to regard anyone with loathing or contempt;
  Never to stop caring.

Help me always to love the sinner, however much I may hate the sin. And help me always to try to understand what makes people act as they do; and help me sometimes to stop and think what I would be like, if I had had as little chance as some of them have had.

  Make me always
    Sympathetic to failure;
    Patient with folly;
    Firm with shiftlessness;
    Stern to cruelty;
    Resolute against those who make vice and evil easier for others.

Help me to be wise enough to know
  When to be kind and when to be stern;
  When to encourage and when to rebuke;
  When to give and when to refuse.
Above all, never let love grow cold within my heart.

Lord Jesus, you came to seek and to save that which was lost, and it is your work that I am still trying to do.

Hear this my prayer for your love's sake. AMEN.

O God, you have set me under discipline. Make me not only at all times obedient to my leaders, but give me the self-discipline which will make me always obedient to the voice of conscience, and to the command of the highest that I know.

Help me always and everywhere to behave in such a way that I will be an honour and a credit to the traditions of my regiment and to the uniform and the badge which I wear.

Bless and protect those whom I love and those who love me, and, when the call of duty separates me from them, keep me true to them and them true to me.

If so it be that some day I must fight, help me to fight only to make peace, only to protect the helpless and the weak, only to support that which is just and right.

Help me at all times to fear you and to honour the Queen.

This I ask for Jesus' sake. AMEN.

A SAILOR'S PRAYER

O God, I ask you to take me into your care and protection along with all those who go down to the sea in ships.

Make me alert and wise in my duties. Make me faithful in the time of routine, and prompt to decide and courageous to act in any time of crisis.

Protect me in the dangers and the perils of the sea; and even in the storm grant that there may be peace and calm within my heart.

When I am far from home and far from loved ones and far from the country which I know, help me to be quite sure that, wherever I am, I can never drift beyond your love and care.

Take care of my loved ones in the days and weeks and months when I am separated from them, sometimes with half the world between them and me. Keep me true to them and keep them true to me, and every time that we have to part, bring us together in safety and in loyalty again.

This I ask for your love's sake. AMEN.

AN AIRMAN'S PRAYER

O God, I thank you that I live in an age in which things that even my father never dreamed of have become commonplace.

I thank you that you have given me the power to travel higher than the clouds and faster than the wind across the sky.

Give me a fit body, a clear eye, a steady nerve and a mind able to make instant decisions.

Protect me in my journeyings, and bring me always safely to my flight's end; and help me,, as I journey far above the clouds in the vast spaces of the sky, to feel your presence near: through Jesus Christ my Lord. AMEN.

A SCIENTIST'S PRAYER

O God, give me in all my work the spirit of reverence.

As I search for the secrets of the universe,
And as I seek to discover nature's laws,
Help me to see behind it all your creative power and purpose.
Help me to love nothing so much as the truth,
And fearlessly to follow wherever truth may lead me.

Give me at all times
The spirit of service,
That I may think and calculate, experiment and search,
Never for power to destroy,
But always for power
To lighten men's burdens;
To feed men's hunger;
To ease men's pain;
To make the world a better place to live in,
Nearer to men's hearts' desire,
And closer to what you meant it to be.

And above all
Give me the humility
Which will make me,
Not proud of what I have discovered,
But conscious of all that I do not know,
And which will always make me think of truth,
Not as something I have found,
But as something which you have given me,
And which must be used
As you would have it to be used.

This I ask for your love's sake. AMEN.

I thank you, O God, for giving me a body which is specially fit and strong, and for making me able to use it well.

In my training
Help me never to shirk the discipline which I know that I need and that I ought to accept.

In my leisure and in my pleasure
Help me never to allow myself any indulgence which would make me less fit than I ought to be.

When I compete with others
Help me, win or lose, to play fair. When I win, keep me from boasting; when I lose, keep me from making excuses. Keep me from being conceited when I succeed, and from being sulky when I fail. And help me always with good will to congratulate a better man who beat me.

Help me so to live that I will always have a healthy body and a healthy mind.

This I ask for your love's sake. AMEN.

A MOTORIST'S PRAYER

O God, every time I drive my car, help me to remember that I am responsible, not only for my own life, but also for the lives of others.

Give me patience, when progress is annoyingly and frustratingly slow, so that I may not endanger my own life and the lives of others by taking a chance to save a minute or two.

Give me courtesy, so that I may think of the other driver as well as of myself.

Keep me always alert, and give me wisdom to know when it is time to stop and rest.

Help me never to indulge in any habit or in any pleasure which would make me a danger to others on the road.

Help me to do everything that one man can do to make life safer on the roads on which I drive: through Jesus Christ my Lord. AMEN.

A TRADESMAN'S
OR A CRAFTSMAN'S
PRAYER

O God, it is you who gave me skill in my hands. You gave me the ability to make wood and metals and the materials out of which things are made obedient to my hands and to my will.

Give me pride in my work. Give me such self-respect that I will always be ashamed to turn out any inferior bit of workmanship or a shoddily done job.

Make me at all times absolutely honest in my work, more concerned to do a job as well as it can be done than with reckoning how much I will get out of it, or how long it will take me to do it.

Help me to work, not to satisfy the clock, but to satisfy my own conscience. Lord Jesus, you were a craftsman in Nazareth, working with the tools of your trade; make me as good a workman as you were.

This I ask for your love's sake. AMEN.

A PRAYER FOR A WRITER,

*an Author, or a Journalist, for all whose craft it is
to use words which many will hear or read*

O God, you gave me the gift and the responsibility of using words. Help me in all my writing and my speaking to be the servant of goodness, of beauty and of truth. Help me never to write or to say anything which would - injure another's innocence or take another's faith away.

Help me never to write or say anything which would make that which is wrong more attractive, or which would soil the mind of anyone who reads or hears it.

Help me never to pander to that which is low, never to seek popularity at the expense of truth, never to be more concerned with sensations than with facts, and always to respect the feelings and the rights of other people.

Grant that all that I write or say be such that it can stand the scrutiny of my own conscience, and such that I could with a clear conscience offer it to you.

This I ask for your love's sake. AMEN.

A PRAYER
FOR ONE WHO IS HELPLESS
OR BED-RIDDEN

O God, life has taken a good deal from me, but I want to begin by thanking you for all that life has left me.

I can see and read; I can hear and listen; I can talk and speak with my friends. Though my body must stay in the one place, I can still send my mind and my imagination in adventurous travel. Once I was too busy doing things to think. Now I can think until I reach you and the things which really matter.

I have still books which I can read, music I can listen to, wireless and television which I can hear and watch, even games which I can play in bed.

For all that, O God, I need your help more than I need anything else. Keep me cheerful even when it is very difficult. Keep me content when my whole being naturally wants to be resentful. Let me not become querulous, complaining, demanding. Keep me from self-pity. Help me to be truly grateful for all that is done for me; and, even when it is the last thing that I feel like doing, help me to smile.

Bless the doctors and the nurses and the people who care for me and who look after me; and give them skill to find a cure some day even for people like me.

When I feel that I am useless and a burden to others, help me to remember that I can still pray, and so help me constantly to uphold the hands of those I love, and constantly to bear them and myself to your throne of grace.

All this I ask for your love's sake. AMEN.

A PRAYER
FOR ONE WHO IS DEAF

O God, life has taken away from me the power to hear, and there is much that I have lost.

I miss the voices of my friends, the music that I loved, the many lovely and homely sounds which others hear.

Sometimes my deafness makes me avoid company, and sometimes it makes things very awkward for me. Sometimes I think that deaf people get less sympathy than anyone else, and that people regard us deaf people as something of a nuisance. It is very easy for a deaf person like me to become lonely and suspicious and to avoid meeting people.

O God, help me to bear it all with a good grace. After all I have got something to be thankful for. I can sleep anywhere, because noise doesn't disturb me, and I can concentrate on my work because sounds don't distract me. When I think about it, I have got some blessings to count!

Help me to do my best to conquer this handicap. Help me at least to be sensible enough to do what I can about it. I thank you very specially for hearing-aids, and for the skill of those who have done so much to help us deaf people to hear.

Help me to do my work and to enjoy my life, even although I cannot hear without my hearing-aid.

This I ask for Jesus' sake. AMEN.

A PRAYER
FOR ONE WHO IS BLIND

O God, I have to live in the dark now, and there is much that I can't help missing.

I can't help missing the faces of my loved ones and my friends, and the colour of the flowers. I can't help feeling it difficult not to see the road that I must walk and the scenes I loved.

O God, help me to face all this with courage and with cheerfulness.

I thank you for all that is done for us blind people. I thank you for books in braille, for guide-dogs wonderfully trained to be wise, for special training to make us able to do a useful job, for the sympathy and the kindness and the consideration which nearly everyone shows to us.

I thank you that my memory has still its gallery of pictures and that the eyes of my mind can still see. Even if I can no longer see the things that are visible, I can still see the things that are invisible.

Keep me from pitying myself, and help me not to let this thing beat me. Help me bravely to train myself to be as independent as it is possible for me to be. I know that no trial ever came to any man without bringing with it the power to bear it. Help me to bear and to conquer this.

This I ask for the sake of him who is the light of the world, for Jesus' sake. AMEN.

A PRAYER FOR ANIMALS

O God, you have made all living things, and you love them all.

Bless all living creatures, especially those in the service and in the homes of men.

Grant that no man may ever be thoughtlessly, callously, or deliberately cruel to the dumb animals who have no voice to speak and no power to defend themselves from the actions of men.

Grant that those who keep animals as pets within their homes may care for them as they ought to be cared for, may never neglect them, or cause them needless suffering and pain.

Bless all animals in captivity, and grant that their masters and their trainers may always be kind.

The animals have given to men their strength and their work, and often even their devotion and their love; grant that men may give to them the care which they deserve as creatures whom your hands have made and for whom your heart cares.

This I ask for your love's sake. AMEN.